LET THE MIDDLEAGED LADY SPEAK

A COLLECTION OF ESSAYS

by

Renée M. Ducker

CreateSpace, North Charleston, South Carolina

2017

ISBN-13 978-0692930496

ISBN-10 0692930493

Dedications

I would like to thank my youngest child, Dr. Tzipporah M. Kormos, Ph.d., for making this book possible. She is my amanuensis in the modern sense of the word. Were she not the highly intelligent, sensitive, intuitive, generous, and technologically savvy person that she is, you would not be reading these words today.

And I would like to thank my husband, Robert Ross Ducker, for coming into my life and being my Rock of Gibraltar.

Foreword

'I have never been politically correct. I say this from the outset, because it will save us a lot of trouble in the long run.' And so starts one of the essays which follow. I'm not endeavouring to either complement or insult you, the reader; I'm merely trying to make you think. If what you read on these pages makes you angry enough to STAND UP AND DO SOMETHING, then I've done my job, IF IT MAKES YOU LAUGH or FEEL HEARTENED ENOUGH TO GET YOU THROUGH YET ANOTHER DAY, then the work was justified, if it does nothing for you at all, then I'll have to try again.

As a writer, I've never been influenced by serial fiction, I want thoughtful writing; I believe both the writer and the reader must work together to achieve something. I'm hoping that I've done something for you AND THAT YOU WILL, now having read my words, DO SOMETHING for society.

As an individual, I've always felt stymied by our controlling society, be it parents all too concerned of what the world would think, teachers who were all too narrow (including several professors much later on), and employers who merely wanted a mindless servant. By middle age one's 'had it' with all that. One's taken all the garbage one can digest and then some, by middle age one wants to say it 'as it is' and let the pieces fall where they may – not to hurt or injure or destroy someone or something – but instead to be one's fuller self, and by middle age (this point in life), as well, one expects not only to be heard but to be listened to.

Many moons ago, when I was in High school, a fellow student asked me if I wanted to help society, why I wanted to be a writer; well folks, if my words motivate you to do something, I have...................

I have chosen not to arrange my essays in a chronological order, allowing the reader to assess each one individually, to see each one's beauty as in a single flower or petal; just as one need not see a painter's work in the order of creation. In many ways what we do is not only the product of the sum total of our existence, but also of the 'nowness' of the situation.

If I've caused you any pain or damage, I apologize, no harm was ever met; after all I am at the heart of everything a Pacifist. Allow my screams and cries to urge you into greater existence and inner meaning; and allow yourself to be a fuller you.

A word about style : as some of these essay have crossed the decades, so the styles you'll find are somewhat varied – the 'excessive' hyphens are to signify free thought (free association) – going from idea to idea – an original pyschoanalytical theory – the 'excessive' commas allow for detailing or poetic breathing space, the spellings (a distant argument with narrow minded professors) are a mixture of current English, Classical European, and my own invention; after all who better than an authour, a wordsmith, to rewrite language.

ENJOY!

In Peace,

Renée M. Ducker

Room 503

Working off and on for the last sixteen months of my life I found I have been granted a most unanticipated gift. Here, I was, trying to find a career more suited to the 'real' me and in between I would do this largely thoughtless boring customer service work, in which my eyes were forced to stare at a computer screen for sometimes, breaks aside, as much as eleven hours a day. And yet amidst the lethargy of the low brow and unintellectual challenge of it all, I was being given a priceless and precious eye view into another world. Now in my other life as a freelance researcher into Comparative Religious Thought, I look (or imagine to look) into other worlds and others' worlds at all times. But this was markedly different. This bird's eye view was neither through literature nor holiday visits to another's place of prayer; this was the actual day by day fly on the wall picture of another world.

You see, except for management and a microcosm group of whites, the bulk of this company workforce are Afro-American or Hispanic, poor Afro-Americans and Hispanics. Having a Human Services/Psych. Background, as I do, one assumes to 'know' what the poor are about. After all isn't that what so many agencies I was trained to work for were designed? Don't we of all people, understand such poor minorities, knowing where 'they come from', how they 'got there' and 'why'? Well, up to sixteen months ago I would have answered a completely thoughtless yes. This was all before the gift.

Let me describe my workplace. Nestled in an unattractive metropolitan office building is a floor of random size offices, without much in the way of decoration, hygiene, or safety considerations. Wires, broken and stained ceiling panels proliferate and mouse droppings are not infrequent. In between all that are tables stocked with computer screens, paraphernalia, telephones, and oh the incidental – the workers. Amidst the barrage of poorly made and maintained technology are the people who work them. Poorly trained and uneducated they come to work to make it 'through' another day.

Let me describe these people, not as we were trained to see them as Human Service Professionals, nor as the public may see them in the news, or movies, or on primetime television, but as they play out their lives in the work world. The people I am describing are real. Their names as well as some of the pictures of the actual company have been changed to protect the innocent; but the view is real.

It is 6:40 am Monday morning. I come into the office, have my fingerprints screened by the time clock, and enter a small and unseemly inner office. It is still dark out but several morning people have beaten me here by several hours. Arising at hours where many night people only start their slumber, they have trained their bodies and minds to ignore the daylight and night darkness rhythms and instead work when their employers instruct them rather than when their bodies and minds would have preferred. One of the workers is an obese Hispanic woman, disabled with a never named condition, which keeps her attached to an intravenal device. She has a preadolescent son, who resides largely with his grandmother, for some unnamed reason; and she in turn, resides with a Hispanic man she has never married and who is not the child's father. She describes her home as in the 'projects', but little more is known about her home life.

The morning continues and gradually more workers walk in the door, allow their fingerprints to be screened and report to an available computer and phone. One dark skinned Afro-American woman in her forties, who can never quite keep to any schedule, comes in and announces that she has to go downstairs for something; as she walks through the narrow, poorly aired room the stench of cigarette smoke fills the air. No worker is allowed to smoke on site, but this woman , Ellie, always smells of it. Coming back ten minutes later she is, as usual, angry at someone or something. Someone held the elevator for another worker, someone was flirting with a supervisor, the guard wasn't watching the 'right' people; her concerns always remain outside herself and her own 'issues'. Sitting down, she immediately is chagrined by her computer seat, after all no one ever holds a 'place' for her. Then, as the phones are slow for the moment, she quickly scans the various computer screens to check up on the other workers to find their errors, print, them and hand them to a supervisor. When another supervisor asks her why she does that, she responds that she's always hearing about 'her' mistakes. Then she gets angry and needs another smoking break.

About twenty minutes later Angela walks in, she's Afro-American as well, but about ten years younger than Ellie. She's also the other side of the rainbow when it comes to personality and perspective. Even with a cold or some personal issue, Angela comes in upbeat, smiling, and accepting. She talks away gaily with her follow workers and with all the issues she has to deal with day by day she laughs and appears to enjoy herself and life as a whole.

Between eight and nine a.m. the small room is filled and the employees are noisily doing their jobs; their work requires constant phone discussion with customers, but the Vice President who sits and stands watch, walking back and forth with all the image of an SS man continues to 'remind' the workers just how loud they are and this he does in a tone far louder than any in the room and with expletives, to boot. This 'distraction' is an everyday occurrence and while viewed as a continual threat to their employment and economic well being, Mr. Jones is hardly viewed with either respect or as the norm in supervision.

It is ten thirty a.m. and most of the morning breaks have been allotted. A morning break is simply a ten minute period of time when the employee is allowed to go to the bathroom, get a drink, or have a smoke. Any movement beyond break time is much discouraged. Then all of a sudden the computer system dies and the employees are forced to take out their white phone pads and take messages, orders, and answer questions without technological assistance. This is always bad news for management as so many messages and clients are lost when this occurs. It's equally bad news for the workers as tremendous pressure is put on them to deal with angry customers without the information they are calling in for and because their few employee 'rights' are immediately removed. Lunches, breaks, even bathroom trips are cancelled during these emergencies. Fortunately this breakdown is short lived, only twenty minutes. The system up again, there's a collective sigh of relief in Room 503.

The lunch time allotments begin and when I return from mine I find several other people have taken the place of the early morning workers. These midday workers tend not to be able to come in for morning shift, and are, in design, supposed to therefore takeover the early evening rush although many of them don't last that long either. Frequently coming in late or disheveled, there is always an excuse or a problem in getting to work or staying the full time. One late adolescent shows up twenty minutes late, without bothering to call in first. His young nineteen years are clouded by his fifteen year old looks. Walking in after noon, he looks as if he has only just awaken and in the few minutes he's been in the room he's lost his key and ipod three times. Clyde is the love of all the Afro-American and Hispanic women there. He is their onsite teddy bear. They baby him and put up with his infantile and irresponsible ways. If he loses something, a daily occurrence, they find it or replace it. If he's late or leaves early they cover for him and if he's broke, which is a continual situation, they 'lend' him money. Money, which is of course never returned. Clyde is a good looking medium skinned Afro-American. He lives with his grandmother, as neither his biological parents seem to take much responsibility for him. He gives some of his sparse salary to his grandmother on a regular basis.

The day slowly passes, afternoon breaks, a mere repetition of the morning break schedule, are allotted and the early evening people slowly appear. Once again, much as in the morning, before any arrival schedule the calls start coming in of absences and anticipated lateness. The early evening crew crawls in, or so it would seem, looking frequently as fatigued as those of us who have put in our lengthy (eight to ten or more hours a day) shifts regardless of whether they have been working or not. Not overly eagerly, they take their places, stopping to speak with the earlier workers, asking if it's been a slow or more demanding day. One dark skinned Afro-American man stands out, he comes in on time daily. This is his second job, he has a clerical civil service position during the day and works late into the night to allow his wife to stay home with the couple's two little girls. He's better educated and spoken than his fellow workers, he's also softer toned in speech, and less jovial. His very facial appearance says 'I'm here to work and nothing else.' The other women don't eye him the way they do the other Afro-American or Hispanic men; he's 'hands off' and not so much because he's married; because married in their parlance is merely one's current living partner, but rather because of 'who' he is. He is not 'one' of them.

I log out of my computer. It is six pm.

Tuesday morning. I arrive a minute earlier than on Monday and once again allow my fingerprints to be screened. Today the machine doesn't respond immediately as programmed and it takes two more tries. Elena, the obese Hispanic woman with the intravenal device is in the process of ordering breakfast. You can always tell the proximity to the last payday by the sparsity or lack thereof of large breakfast orders. It's only Tuesday and by the size of her three course breakfast order, it is apparent that there's still money in her account. The general order always consists of high fat, highly salted, and highly caloric items. Fruits and vegetables are largely ignored except as garnishes. Highly sugared drinks are also usually the rule of the day.

As the clock tics closer to 7:30 am, a large white woman walks in. Everyone immediately moves his or her chair to allow her weight around them. She doesn't look happy; she's been moody and irritable for several weeks since her online romance ended. Besides the grimace, replacing the former half smile, the irritability takes its form in an ongoing spat with Elana, Mary either makes a snippy remark, ignores her, or talks about her as is she weren't there. This morning, she just merely walks all around the room, as people rapidly move in the inch or two their seating situations will allow, and then picks herself up and situates herself in the outside room. Elana will then continue to remark on Mary's behavior and demeanor for the remainder of her working day.

Its eight o'clock and the office is filling. The supervisors have arrived and the V.P., cheerless despot that he is, is seated on his throne. Anita strolls in. Indeed Anita always strolls; timeliness never seems to occur to her. Anita is an anorexic looking Haitian-Afro American. Daddy provided the Afro-American side and Mommy the Haitian and Creole language. Anita is an interesting mixture of unleashed fury and immaturity. She lacks any of the normal deference to work superiors, rules, or scheduling and on the other hand when anxious, Anita sits quite unabashedly thumb fully inserted in her mouth in plain view of everyone. She also is known for her inability to sit still as she runs aimlessly from one free seat in one office to another. Coming from a poor family and never managing to make it through an entire scheduled week of employment, Anita is always complaining of being 'short'. Yet she's always buying clothing, jewelry, cds, and fast food.

The morning crawls on and the morning breaks pass and the usual doldrums of the slowing of the morning calls occur. In design, this permits the employees to read up on the communications lines which list new accounts, problem areas, and the ever stinging disciplinary comments and threats. It is here that full time employees are reminded that they can lose their medical benefits, something they pay for at around twenty percent of their weekly paychecks, if they are not keeping to their full schedules. It's where employees are repeatedly chastised for lack of punctuality, spelling errors, and frequent ignoring of account instructions. On a rare occasion praise from some customer is added, but this is always rare. The irony of the multitude of barbed comments on this twice daily read listing, is that the entire system, including the listing, is full of spelling, grammatical, and instructional errors. This is to say nothing of the full ignorance of any labor laws or humanitarian considerations.

The call pace picks up and lunch time allotment time arrives. Once again the flurry of fast food appears and I leave to seek some lunchtime air. When I return the room is in a tizzy. The dark skinned Afro-American supervisor in the far office has printed up error reports on almost everyone in the room. The reports are the usual singled out spelling errors, from a supervisor who frequently uses ain't in his own communications and cannot differentiate council from counsel or affect from effect; fortunately he rarely has to deal with these vocabulary issues. In one way this type of correction is exactly what Alexander is paid to do; on the other, the errors he chooses to document are frequently more indicative of his needing to feel superior rather than improving a customer service product or educating an employee. Dictionaries are available for employee usage, as Spell Check is not; but as any good teacher knows individuals who really do not know how to spell do not know when they are spelling a word correctly or not.

The afternoon slowly passes. The president starts making an announcement as the employees are busy on the phones; it is always amazing to watch this management faux pas, as the employees are supposed to be helping clients and listening to management simultaneously. The emergency this time is yet another client complaint. It seems that an employee read messages over the phone to a client without requesting a password. It would be easier were the process standardized so that every client had a password; but this is never considered. It is merely just another problem to pass onto the employees as not only 'their' problem but as their fault as well.

A new buzz is in the air; as word of another firing is passed on. This time it's a part time city college student. This particular sullen gay Hispanic late adolescent calls out every few weeks for lengthy absences and even when he does come in is rarely, if ever, on time. He also is not known for handling many calls. Any firing produces quiet or not so quiet employment fears into the general atmosphere. Discussions immediately erupt as to the appropriateness of this particular firing. Any employee loss is compared to past employee firings and frequently current or past employees seen as errant, or more errant are cited as more appropriate candidates. The day has ended with a bad taste in the collective employee mouth.

It is six o'clock.

Wednesday is an abysmal morning. It is pouring, windy, and flooding out. Even the normally punctual employees prove to be late, a lateness that can repeatedly be held even against 'good' employees as far as the denial of any earned daily bonus for that week based on even a single weather caused lateness.

The calls appear heavier whenever there are less available operators and 8:30 am comes around fast.

Faun appears shortly after the half hour mark. Faun is a newly twenty-one year old overweight Hispanic female. Her ample bosom immediately peers over her array of revealing shirts. When it becomes annoying she adjusts her shirts, if not she proceeds as if unknowing or uncaringly. Although, grammar and spelling ignorant, Faun is a hard worker and appears brighter than her limited academic knowledge allows. Early on it was apparent to the supervisors that Faun cared and could be counted on to answer the calls and do a decent job of it. But apparently the same dysfunctional family that kept her from completing an Associates degree in the city community college, would also prevent her from securing a more desirable work record. Every morning it would be something different, one day it would be a prescription that she had to pick up for her grandmother first, another it would be the change of daily schedule she had to request to insure her mother medical help. Then there was the Sunday morning that she showed up after having been robbed of all her available cash by her sister's 'friends'. For a young unmarried woman she is already emotionally and physically, if not officially financially, supporting a family. Today she comes in excuseless, finds her earphones hidden in a cabinet, and takes a seat. Looking over to the room supervisor, Faun smiles and inquires as to when the morning breaks are starting............"I'm hungry", she says. Everyone looks around the room and agrees to let her go first. Hunger is not ignored in the room. It's understood, felt, and respected everyday. Whether it means a sparsely filled refrigerator, or living in a single room where there are no kitchen privileges and food means fast food three times a day, or because there were too many other expenses this week and food had to wait…..hunger looms large here. Sometimes alternate money management comes to mind as when one Afro-American woman one day commented that maybe if she hadn't purchased that carton of cigarette, to say nothing of the recreational drugs, that she could have bought some chicken or "something".

Faun returns from her break with a large croissant filled with egg, cheese, and sausage. She immediately complains that there's too much egg. Drowning her breakfast with a soft drink, Faun covers her ear with the earphone and goes back to work.

The morning crawls slowly by and my lunch break comes. I arrive back to a lively discussion on the current city political scene. There have been a lot of televised ads and these are a television absorbed lot. I'm interested to see what they make of the campaign dialogue. Angela mentions that she likes the Hispanic candidate, after all, she states that the white guy is a millionaire, what could he possibly know about the needs of the poor city residents. In addition he's Jewish and we all know that "Jews run the world" as is.

Fauns mentions another candidate's name, but his name is "silly" she stammers; how could anyone vote for someone with a name like that?! Clyde has arrived, late as usual, he mentions how wonderful

Roosevelt had been for the poor, getting them jobs and benefits. That "Teddy" he exclaims was a "real" president. No one present in the room knows enough to correct his mistake and the afternoon crawls on.

Evening approaches with no major interruption except for the usual name announcements on the overhead intercom system when an employee has a call. In the operators' cases it's usually collection agencies or a needy family member. Phone calls don't bring smiles to these operators. There's no feigned embarrassment or surprise, just chagrined misery. Another bill that can't be paid, at least on time, or a child requiring immediate pick up, or a close relative requiring money or accommodations. All this amidst management's repeated warnings on operators receiving calls, especially on certain earmarked lines, or frequently at all.

The sky darkens and finally the clock reads six o'clock.

Thursday dawns dark and miserable, even before entering the squalid office, I am met with persistent coughing, both Elana and Mary are coughing nonstop. I allow my fingerprints to be screened, hoping against hope that I somehow fail to contract this bout of flu or colds.

The dark skies persist and the morning crew walks in shivering. Angela has tissues filling her nostrils, I gently enquire as to whether she had a bad nosebleed or an accident. Angela, ever the jovial, shakes her head no – she has a bad cold and she can't get her "nose to stop running". Besides health issues, the inappropriate lookingness of the 'cure' never dawns on her.

Faun appears and seeing Angela's illness borne situation, tells the room her emergency room story for the nth time. On one of Faun's days off, she ended up in the emergency room. Having had a localized rash, and neither knowing its genesis nor its cure, she elected to having it seen by a local Emergency Room physician. She fails to add that she had also chosen to ignore Clyde's 'enlightened' advice of just pouring bleach on it; "works on everything", he proudly advised. Five hours after entering the City Hospital, Faun left; never being seen by the doctor. There had been apparently one emergency after the other, and while the nurse kept trying to sooth Faun with "he'll be with you soon"; after five hours Faun had enough. No word on when or if the rash also left.

Bridget appears at the time. Bridget is little older than Faun. She is a very dark skinned Afro-American single mother. Her four year old daughter, Barbara, fills her continual conversations, with the difficulties of raising a very demanding youngster on an impossibly low income. Bridget exhibits an insect bite on her forearm today. She complains to the room at large that it won't stop itching and that she doesn't know what to do with it. One supervisor suggests rubbing alcohol. She responds agreeably that that "sounds like a good idea" and maybe she should try that with Barbara, too. No one appears concerned or shocked that this impoverished young woman doesn't even have enough basic medical knowledge to treat a child's, to say nothing of her own, insect bites.

The morning passes, and as I leave for my lunch break, Clyde arrives, needing money. He is disheveled, tired and irate looking. He had apparently gone to one of the local take out food places only to find that the dollar he was certain that he had in his pocket was no longer there. Faun reaches into her wallet and finds three dollars for the man-boy. He then announces that he's too sick to work and leaves. No one comments on the absurdity of not working when one needs the money so badly. One supervisor shakes her head and I walk out of the office, eager for outside air.

When I return Susie is sitting at the other side of the narrow room. She is coughing nonstop. She explains, in between wheezed breaths, that she is Asthmatic. The supervisor comments, in her earshot, that she's "a smoker with the flu". Taking phone calls as she goes, Susie's productive coughs fill the room. Several operators from the outside office take a peek in to view the office patient. One white afternoon/evening supervisor remarks out loud on our "Typhoid Mary". No one adds the comment that without any company sick days at all (only management, which is salary plus perk based, has sick days) how could Susie afford to lessen her already meagre pay.

The afternoon crawls at a snail's pace as I agonize on the office illness patterns. Some of us do wipe down our keyboards; but the bulk of the operators even share their earphones as they cannot remember to bring them back and forth from home to work everyday and there are no lockers or private cubby spaces to keep them.

Its six 0'clock, hoping that my throat itch is merely an allergic reaction to the continual smoke stench, I allow my fingerprints to be screened and hurry out into the air.

Its Friday morning, payday; the day I have renamed Petty Cash Day. The collective office mood is always lifted on Friday and life's never ending miseries seem less trying, less burdensome on that day.

I allow my fingerprints to be screened and I walk into the little office. The sole male employee at that time, Johnny, a gay, white unemployed actor with a suicidal background, greets me with "Guess what isn't in our accounts yet?" He is referring to the direct deposits which most of the employees currently have. I figure that his bank is just late and I ignore the issue, smiling and endeavouring to calm him and just get down to work. Elana and Mary show up within the next half hour with the same hapless news. I check in on my own account at my usual 8:30 and find that my direct deposit, too, has not arrived. Not happy with the situation, either, I too find myself checking and rechecking the account over the next hour. The office fills with the morning staff, who quickly hear the news whether they have checked their accounts or not. Faun mentions that she knew right away when she couldn't pay for her weekly subway train ticket this morning; fortunately, she adds, that she had "$2.00 left to cover the morning ticket. I woulda had to go back home," she adds.

Circa 10:30 am with the phones ringing steadily both from clients on business calls and off duty employees seeking information as to where their direct deposits were, management makes a very quiet statement. The quietness of the tone is striking considering the decibel level of their usual nonstop scoldings. "The bank made a mistake," we are told. Our direct deposits will not be in our accounts until Saturday, Monday "At the latest." No one says anything; partially because they're busy handling customer queries and partially due to the collective powerlessness that is always there, now heightened by the situation.

A day to half a week later is no small dilemma to employees who may not have carfare home, to say nothing of money to meet their grocery needs or cover the checks that went out with the assurance of direct deposit. No one considers the possible responsibility of the employer/bank to cover returned check fees. Everyone is busy figuring how they're going to make it through to Saturday or Monday. Once again the Despotic V.P, whispers that if anyone requires emergency funds to cover them until the direct deposits are received can see the Comptroller. They are forewarned that the amounts will have to be "reasonable". Considering the tight budgets that these employees operate under, whether or not they can keep to a budget, 'reasonable' is almost a joke. Faun mentions that she was going to take one of her brothers out for his birthday. "How can I do that now," she asks out loud "is that reasonable?" Picturing management carrying on life as usual, my inside voice, says "Damn straight.!" But I keep this witticism to myself.

While it's true that many seemingly affluent individuals live very much up to the line, that they could not go through a month paying their mortgage without their anticipated steady income; but that being said, they also have credit cards and lines of credit and imposing personalities which say hold that check and don't deposit it 'Until I say to.' I remember sitting on a city bus one morning, with another destination in mind. The seemingly affluent woman next to me had apparently lost her checkbook and wallet. She was having a well televised cell phone conversation with her bank. "I don't care what your policy is", she demanded. "You are not doing anything until I get there and I have a 10:30 meeting to attend first." You can rest assured that that woman's checks were not returned.

The usual uplift of Friday has paled. In lieu of heavy lunch orders and lunchtime spending sprees, there are quiet trips to the Comptroller, where everyone is humbled into asking for less than she or he needs and everyone is nervous about its repayment. My Friday schedule is only till 12:00 noon. I usually wish everyone a 'Great Weekend' at that point; but I feel strangely guilty. How can you wish a bunch of people who looked forward to their momentary wealth all week long and instead were left with further debt and disillusionment. As is, wishing people a good weekend, who frequently work through at least part of the weekend, has always been a dilemma for me; but how much greater so when this movie-going-party-loving gang has been denied their movies and partying for at least this pay period. I murmur a quiet

"Good Weekend" and hurry out into the cold but sunny air. It would prove to take me well into my lengthy ride home to simmer down from the miserable feeling that had congealed in that office that day. And mine was just the misery of witnessing; those people, those Elanas, and Bridgets, and Fauns, and Angelas, and even Clydes were going to have to live with it and as it was to turn out – until Monday.

A.M. Safety Warnings

Having watched children - our children - your children disembark the school/camp bus for the last eighteen years of my life, I've come to feel I've noticed a few conspicuous changes over the years. Oh, more than fads - like - let's say 'poodle skirts are gone'! No, I've noticed a much more child controlled dress arriving on my doorstep each day. Oh, this is far more than 'Everyone's wearing them short this year, Mom" or "Everyone wears jeans to school". No, this is more like Mom's not home, so I leave the house without my coat, or I like my skirt long and even though I'm only seven and going to trip - "I'm going to WEAR IT anyway!!!"

My words here are not to sit in judgment of you, the busy working mother, but rather to leave you to question the wisdom involving letting jr./miss run the house - even if you look at it as only fashion - or maybe even only school/camp. Furthermore, I too was a working mother, albeit usually within view of my youngsters, but nonetheless, full time working mother. Let it suffice for me to say that it is readily easy to pick out those children whose parents do not direct their preschool (being prior to school and not necessarily nursery school) doings. These are the children wearing short sleeves and no coats on twenty-five degree days or conversely long sleeved woolly turtlenecks on balmy seventy-five degree ones. Once again I am not here as an AUTHORITY, but rather an experienced professional, who after picking fallen children off the sidewalk, or helping others to pull up fallen sweaters or lunch bags, have a few words to add ease and yes - that word AGAIN - safety to your child's school/camp day.

My first word to guide you is development - is your child developmentally ready to remember his/her own lunch, proper over-clothing items, and other school supplies. If you're not really sure and he/she is below nine, the answer is probably NO!!!! In addition, the young child, unencumbered by supervision, will be sure to take her/his favorite poseable figure/stuffed toy or computer game in addition or stead of his/her real necessities.

How would I even begin to know this, you wonder - well each morning for the last eighteen years I have seen these little ones emerge from bus/carpool with an armful of supplies - "Well, you say - "Teachers' orders!" Hardly - an adequate description of an armful of Barbie dolls. Then much to everyone's chagrin, as the child ambers on into school - all of a sudden - little Amy's back at my feet again - crying "I forgot my lunch/backpack/note at home - well of course, where was there room with all those Barbies per cubic space....... In addition, for these little guys - hoods are great - they protect from wind, rain, and cold - umbrellas are problematic. Easily until a child is ten or eleven - your child's cries of requiring an umbrella should fall on DEAF EARS. Indeed, even with these supposed safety ones - a young child has more than enough to hold, open and close today - without the accompaniment of yet another object to lose or accidentally (and sometimes not so) hurt his/her classmate.

Beyond development - there's always fashion. It seems the neighbor's child is always wearing THAT. Well, I must say, I always cavalierly replied "I don't care" - however, if that

UNDERSTANDABLY is not you - try "Its not safe Darlin'!" You CAN always revert to 'I'm the parent' if need be........... Fashion when I went to elementary school was far neater, practical and REGULATED by school rules... Now with Jimmy and Jinny ruling - we have to review fashion. This does not necessitate a visit to Vogue or the Times Fashion Issue - NO, only to commonsense! Does it provide needed coverage of exposed body parts, is it weather correct, does it fit, is it comfortable, COULD IT CAUSE AN ACCIDENT????? The last one is harder than one would think....... One bus company sent home a notice requesting NO DRAW STRING JACKETS - why - were they selling a competitor's number - NO - because in their experience, the draw strings had caused children to be stuck on door handles, seat belts, one another, etc., etc... Are the pants/skirts so long that they would cause tripping? Are the sleeves so long that the child has to continually push them up dropping other needed items SIMULTANEOUSLY? Is the new fad pants which zip mid, lower, or upper leg to become SHORTS? Have you ever watched children unzip them and continue to walk around with the lower half draped over their sneakers? And a word or two about footwear - IS IT FASHIONABLE OR SAFE???? Why does an elementary girl need heels, clogs, or slippery plastic sandals to slide or trip over??? Are sneakers, sneakers if they're so high that they bring your daughter/son up to the ninety-fifth percentile?

Even adolescent and pre-adolescents require some supervision - the greater likelihood - THESE DAYS - is that if it's cool it is NOT SAFE!!!!! Who ever expected wheels on sneakers?????????????? OR Boots designed to accentuate leg curves but NOT PROTECT FROM THE RAIN OR SLIPPERY ICE????????????????

Safety on the carpool/bus also leads to belongings - how much is you child carrying, what, for what reason, and in what? Oh, I know I've read those NOW NOTORIOUS warning of how all those overpacked bookbags are causing back problems - I'll leave that judgment up to you - however HEAR ME OUT!!!! If your child's backpack is overfilled - is it ever emptied - Are all the items required by the school (or just the child)? Secondly, if you ever saw six year olds handle these new wheeled backpack/suitcases - YOU'D DIE!!!!!!! WHY? Because he/she can't - they trip over them or get them stuck in between the seats of the bus/carpool van....... They hit other students trying to control this out-of-control-nightmare.........No, perhaps your middle school/high schooler requires one (PERHAPS) - BUT YOUR LITTLE ONE DOES NOT!!!!!!!!!!!!!!!!!!!!!!!!!!!!

The more your child is carrying out the door in the morning, the more likely items are to be lost, ruined, or cause tripping - teach your child organizational skills - by insisting lunches, notes, loose leaves all HAVE TO FIT in our BAG!!!!!!!!!!!!!! Under most regular circumstances - if the child can't carry it - he/she shouldn't have to bring it - THOSE NASTY SCHOOL PROJECTS ASIDE (YOU SHOULD TRY TO BRING IT IF the student can't - YEAH - YOU ARE THE PARENT!!!!)

What then is the early to work / late coming home parent to do then......... The child needs supervision. Well, if one parent/much older sibling is home - he/she must be taught to supervise - if the nanny/au pair/ housekeeper/ babysitter/grandparent is there, that individual, TOO, MUST BE TAUGHT TO SUPERVISE. Having seen nasty gashes occurring over needless tripping - the effort to supervise might save you a

nasty trip to the emergency room. And, oh well, let's bring back

those poodle skirts - I never remember them hurting anyone!!!!!!!!!

Bereft of the Holidays

What do holidays mean to us? Oh, be careful how you answer, because holiday for the British means vacation, as in 'I'm going on holiday'. No, I mean holidays - those religious, national, familial, and greeting card events which we hold near and dear to our hearts.

Some of us don't think a lot of about them at all. So many holidays have simply become three day weekends on the American scene, almost leaving the remembrance for which they had been entitled, behind. Others, are days which may have had greater significance to former generations, either historically or religiously, and now leave us cold; buying a paper poppy from a Veteran on Memorial Day or sending a card on a cousin's birthday.

And yet holidays are part of the very fabric which keeps us woven together; making up the woof and tweed of our very existence and heritage. They keep us connected to our European aunts and fellow Iowians. They are neither as superficial, nor as business generated weekend longators, as they may appear.

Years, decades, and centuries ago the holidays you celebrated, or equally shunned, were merely by virtue of your religion or your geographic residence, not so much a matter of choice, but rather birth or migration. Today, you are as likely to be of another faith as your uncle Charlie, and of a wholly different political persuasion as your neighbor. So this year when you are asked to work on Thanksgiving; what's the big deal? "Hey, man, it's just Turkey Day! I can always buy another turkey!" True, you can always buy another turkey or even keep the one the supermarket gave you frozen – until next time; but does that truly render the traditional American Pilgrim holiday just another day? What about Father's Day, your wife or girlfriend's birthday, or Christmas? When does something actually mean more to us than a Hallmark occasion?

When earlier groups of immigrants joined our great land, they too brought their holidays with them. This was before Hallmark or Kodak were holiday insigne. The holidays these people carried in their back rolls, valises, and heads had been with them since time immemorial. Indeed when many religious Jews came to this country, they had to deal with their holidays, in what for many, would become a live or die approach. Do I work on these spiritual days, or do my family and I, go without shelter, food, and clothes? It was not a gentle decision. This was indeed how the Conservative Jewish movement was conceived.

And yet many today could never see themselves as fighting such a gut wrenching inner battle. The dollar and cents end answers the questions. Holidays are largely rearranged for business and government ease. If I work today, I can take a longer weekend in a fortnight, etc., etc., etc..

And what does it really matter after all. Isn't it just another day – aren't they all just fancy names for archaic notions, either historical or religious? I sat silent in an office full of African American low level clerical workers. These women barely have a high school diploma between them, functional illiterates, unable to spell, or read anything of meaning. And yet they had very strong opinions. 'Christmas is just a day when couples break up because the guy is pushed too hard to buy the girl a gift.' 'Why would anyone tell a kid that Santa Claus brought the gifts when they went broke buying them themselves?' 'What does Thanksgiving have to do with me?'

One doesn't have to be impoverished or uneducated to have given up on the traditional holiday wealth, however; the young attorney in the law firm, doctor in the medical practice, or newbie in the business, too, are manipulated to give up their holidays as the first step up on their professional ladders. For many there is no big question; money is money. Perhaps they've no emotional attachments at that time, so what's the big deal. It's just another day. BUT IS IT?

In the last three years of my life I went from working in a school where vacations and holidays are a given; to an extremely cheap customer service business where nothing is given. Employees are coerced, manipulated, and threatened; holidays do not exist there – you ignore the world and work. Just as the immigrants came here and largely gave up their holiday inheritance in order to survive, the people in this work world are intimidated to work regardless of all else. Holidays, much like family members, are needless attachments which only get in the way of work assignments.

Much as I never expect much of landlords, other than to collect the rent, I expect nothing more from employers. The former make their living on your requiring a habitat, the latter on the labor you exert in order to pay that landlord. Neither sees you as their source of income, but rather as an inconvenient attachment. Employers insist their staffs work on days rich in meaning for them and landlords, strangely, will finally send out a repairman on the one day of the year that the family is together in peace and prayer. This is no accident. This is an assault on

the American society; this is an assault on the individual and his

freedoms.

When many religious Jews gave up their holidays and Sabbaths

in order to survive, it was not lightly. It frequently occurred after losing

job after job, home after home. It wasn't with a shrug or a nod and a

wink. They knew only too well what they were leaving behind; and few

felt that it would ever be recovered. Conservative Judaism grew out of

this painful, practical dilemma. Jews would have to be Jews, when they

could, where they could, in order to survive. It would take close to

another century until Orthodox Jewry would fight its way to Sabbath and

holiday freedom.

In taking stock at the many hardships that have chipped away on

my life in the last few years, it has only recently come to me that not the

least of them is my loss of the holidays. These days, be it religious or

national, there is a better chance that I am working than not, that I am

alone, rather than with loved ones, and that I have lost the wealth of the

time to remember why the day is not just another day. I had been aware

that my understanding, appreciation of the calendar had dwindled, but

not that my whole connection was terminally ill. No one had ever warned me, that as I gave up day after day, once imbued with deep

meaning, that I would be giving up more than my memories, but rather

an integral part of my life. Who wouldn't be depressed?

I have often taught that anger, when it serves to get you up to

change your life, is purposeful. In this case, I'm hoping that this holiday

depression can serve the same slot. If I am truly bereft of all those

special days, then surely, I must take them back – or at least those of

which I feel the pain of loss. I must do this to resurrect my humanity.

Just as I once added work hours and days to pay the rent and feed my

stomach; now it has become time to give up much of it to feed my soul.

Surely this is a bill that cannot be paid any too soon.

Boxes

It seems to be that the coldness in the world, in which we find ourselves, can be largely explained away by our use of boxes.

Look at the young mothers of our generation. They hold their babies, not in their arms, not on their hips, but largely in an expensive modernistic contraption called a carseat. I call it a box. It holds, encases, and encages the youngster. The warmth that would have been exchanged by the skin to skin contact, that holding a child would demand, is gone. The contact is the mother's skin to plastic and the child's skin to plastic.

I remember in the days prior to such madness, my midwife and I argued over the coming legislation demanding that all young child be ensconced in these plastic devices. I argued, then, that it was cold and I wasn't buying the safety angle. In the end the legislation went through. It was almost laughable that following the enactment, it came out that the safety results weren't anywhere near as foolproof as the legislation backers had publicized.

But let's spend a moment looking a little closer, at what's really at stake here. You conceive a child and from second one, the world, largely through the medical community, but also, in addition to an ever growing set of social laws, cufflinks your relationship to this growing life. Doctors, hospitals, and the government will dictate how your pregnancy is handled, where and how you deliver, and everything thereafter. Now, before you say that maybe they know more than you, maybe it's in my unborn child's better interest; maybe your better think about it. First of all, what is natural about this pattern? Secondly, what makes those in power necessarily all knowing; why are we permitting them to play G-d? Thirdly, how far would you like this to go? Surely, the next step is to control conception as well. Do you truly want to conceive under the watchful eye of the medical and governing community; somehow I doubt it.

No doctor, no governing body, can ever promise you complete safety anyway; no matter what statistics they'd like to quote. There is also a quality of life issue here. How well is life lived, when it is so directed; when you carry your child about plastic to plastic, rather than skin to skin.

In Denmark, with it's long background in Socialism, the government even has the last word on naming the child. It has been known to take as much as six months to 'okay' the parent's choice of name. The excuse given is that, otherwise, parents might pick names causing the child problems. Perhaps, but aren't the parents, the parents? Can't those who conceived the child, even choose its name?

An old friend and colleague told the story of when after he and his wife experienced a multiple birth, the hospital staff seriously canvassed their vehicle making certain that the carseats were perfectly secured. As he said, not tongue in cheek at all, here they were so very worried about the carseats. But were they worried that the children would be well taken care of, fed, or have a safe place to lay their heads?

When we insist on making social legislation, we have to ask ourselves what makes us so 'smart' that we should be ruling others' lives? I, personally, am not thrilled with homseschooling, but that fact is external schooling doesn't work for everyone. I completely dislike many parenting styles, but there are many different types of people out there. I worry about the mentally ill and intellectually deficient; but I don't feel that means we should lock them up or drug them up the kazoo. I'm one person. Each government is one government. Before we dictate, we better be darn sure that there's no other way to insure safety.

When I was having my children, there was a witch hunt going on against midwives. The medical community was terrified that they would be losing a bloody fortune; so they went after midwives. My midwives are no long practicing; and women lost the use of many, many more. Today, thanks to some gutsy women, midwifery is back. The medical community would like to brainwash you to the safety of traditional gynecological/obstetrical care. But if you take a gamble of what that buys you today, you would be flabbergasted by the endless tests involved. No one seems to be questioning their safety. Or how about the tremendous dangers of hospital error and the contagion of hospital diseases. No one seems to be questioning that. This is to say nothing of the endless cutting of women in the form of episiotomies and Cesarean Sections. Are these, too, unquestionable?

Seems to me, given my druthers, I'd rather die in the arms of my mother than in a cold, plastic box. Boxes after all, are traditionally looked at as symbolizing coffins. Why are we boxing our children anyhow?

The Circle That is Life

When I think of my earliest days of mature thinking, that is days marked with mature ideas regardless of age, I remember a young person intent on thinking for herself. I think of a daring approach to life characterized with a belief in G-d, the individual, caring for others, and free thinking. In the circular journey that makes up life, I can now visualize that path I took from those early musings and how I returned to where I am today.

Each individual is a complex connection of parts. Each part can set the same person off in a different direction. I, being human, am no different.

The independence directed me to leave an unhappy home of origin both precociously and precariously early. The free thinking with its growing link of love of knowledge would lead me to a life long pursuit of reading, intellect, and the practical and creative arts; this all in spite of or maybe even because of the early disillusionment with standard educational processes, a belief in itself which would permeate my life in practice and thought. The caring for others would also remain a lifetime pursuit as it wardrobed itself in different roles throughout my lifetime. The belief in the All Mighty also took on different colours in different ages or life stages.

The last director, is especially interesting to follow as it directed my actions in various life stages. In its earliest seedlings it led me to read about my family's Judaism, something that was almost frowned on in my biological family base. It led me to look in on my friends' religious experiences, something my family hated even more. And then, paired with the supreme independent streak, I married young into a religious Born Again/Bible Baptist family. That they were, in addition, abusive, ignorant, and alcoholic, was at that time beyond my naïve eyesight. All and all, it was that interesting combination of parts that led me on the adult journey of leaving my childhood home.

I would remain in that lifestyle for only several years, leaving me with my first child, my growing love for the independent pursuit of knowledge, and my respect for religion. In my next life step I would once again, as I had tried in my childhood home, embrace the Judaism that I had know from my family only in name. This embracement would lead to my second marriage. The man, a not unintelligent, but cowardly mother's boy, with a cruel, miserly, and selfish family would lead me,

although surely he himself was incapable of being anything but a

follower, into several decades of organized Orthodox Judaism, largely

without him; as he had retreated back to his family – which he in a real

sense never left.

During those two decades I, left to rear, my now three children,

very much on my own, grew measurably in all areas. My independence

allowed me to see my sole adultness as a positive, to take stances and

make decision for myself and my family by myself. My caring for others

proved a natural in my adopted religious community; one role following

the other. My role as a wage earner never would prove pleasing to me;

but I was often able, against employer wishes, to play caretaker of many

a soul. This would always provide me with a feeling of accomplishment

looking back on a frequently unhappy working history. I continued my

reading and eventually would gain access to an atypical educational

program which would allow me to matriculate into a more traditional

professional status holder. It would prove to be my beliefs in the

individual and free thought, that the religious community at large could

neither make room for nor provide support, that would cause me to

gradually exit stage right from the community that had housed, fed, and

loved me for so long. Like fair-weather friends, they had, by in large, proved to love only those who questioned not and followed blindly. The make up of my parts, had made that association impossible, from day one.

My exit, like most planned exits, was slow. First, my having to put my youngest child in a school for the gifted led to my almost excommunicated status, then moving to a less right wing Jewish community left me even less amoured as they were a largely materialist community devoted to the dollar rather than G-d or humanity. During this time period, I would be focusing my research into comparative religious thought into a lifetime study. Gradually I would come to buy more works, take notes, and carve that into my real career along with my writing, not a career where I earned wages, but one granting me my personhood – my soul.

In developing my new life force, not a new personality directive, but a force born of the existing ones, I eventually left my longterm employment of misery only to join yet another one. The greatest difference being that the former one demanded feigning right winged adherence, the latter only the love of the mighty dollar. I refused to do either. I stay employed only to pay my bills and nothing more.

The life wheel goes on and as I watch my own children emerge as ever fuller adults. I look for signs of me in them, as well as what makes them who they are, in themselves. The eldest, as I write, has chosen to stay apart from me for quite sometime. The middle, with all her limitations, is a mother and teacher and hopefully still growing. The youngest, my once precocious child, emerges as a budding scientist with an independent and free thinking flare; I hope to be able to see at least a glimpse of where it takes her while I still am on this earth.

My disability, a lifelong part of me, now far worsened, born not of mind but body, grows in its degree of dictations – read limitations - on my existence. Once a fact, I could quietly acknowledge and put on a backburner, she now stands up straight not allowing you to miss her. I've never seen her as an outside existence; I do mind the encroachment of my lifestyle and lifestyle choices. Until her takeover, I felt able to climb tall mountains in a single bound, an earthly Super Woman, if you will. Now it sometimes takes my whole will just to get up for work or even to muster the energy for something I love; yet and nonetheless I see myself as being able to do those things I desire most. Although it will take more of my fierce independence and freethinking spiritual directives to do so, I will continue to conquer my life road ahead.

And I, as I look back over the last fifty some odd years on this circle of a lifetime, I am more who I was at the outset than ever. The circle, it would appear takes you through a lifetime of experiences; and should you survive, allows you to emerge, not unchanged, not unmolested, not even necessarily unloved, but very much who you were at the outset is who you are at the end.

Daughters' Day

Perhaps it should really be Daughters' Day.

I'm not a success because I'm a mother,

But because you're my daughters.

The sun sets, flowers lose their petals,

Birds fly away;

But as a Mother and a Writer,

I will always have you and my words.

Today,

When I look at my life,

I realize how incredibly fortunate I have been,

Because you're mine.

The Decision

There are some decisions that plague you with questions and what ifs. They keep you up nights, tossing and turning, sometimes even after the decision has been made. Others appear crystal clear, almost as if there was no decision to be made at all. This is about the latter variety, for although I thought about it and the idea of turning it down weighed heavily upon my chest; for me there really was no decision. Through my eyes, it was merely a matter of wrong and right – opportunity versus catastrophe.

The scene took place some twelve years ago. The little girl it whirled about, is now an accomplished young woman. I always have to remind myself of that fact when I look back upon that time, that place in space; that it was indeed quite some time ago.

My youngest daughter, like her siblings, went to the Orthodox Yeshivah in which I taught. For her siblings, attending that school had, largely, been a good decision. They got along well with their classmates and the teachers worked well for them. My youngest daughter, was very much her own person though, from kindergarten on, in that peculiar institution, it was the rare teacher who knew what to do with her. True, she had nice friends, but most of them would never go half as far as she academically and almost all allowed much, if not all, their decisions to be made for them.

Tzippi, always knew her own mind. At birth, the midwife wanted her to wake up and nurse; she wanted to sleep. She got up in her own good time, giving me a priceless unforgettable smile, and nursing, then, on her own terms. Tzippi, never had to be kept busy; she always found something worthwhile to do. As a toddler, she would awaken her neurologically impaired sister from a pathological sleep and get her up and playing. While the other girls played jump rope and made mud pies in kindergarten, she dug for dinosaurs. But a Yeshivah, like many other institutions, saw everything in very simple terms and so very early on there was an uneasy relationship between the institution, teachers, Tzippi, and myself.

By middle school age, the uneasiness had become unbearable, first Tzippi, would become depressed and then physically ill; there was no longer a choice.

Several miles away, in a rather sophisticated community, there was a well known highly respected prep school. It was known, as not only a school of the most capable student, but of the artist, and the unique thinker. We applied.

The school in which I taught, charged approximately five or six thousand a year for tuition, in those days; the new institution about twelve. Moreover, in the Yeshivah, my employeeship largely covered my children's tuition; here, I would be quite on my own. In addition, the head of the Yeshivah, in the frequent manner of the far right, where everything is decided for you, as in most religions, did everything to stop the change in academic venue. His tardiness in turning over the records, may well have cost her the sorely needed scholarship, for what would turn out to be her first year there.

Tzippi placed top on the school's admission test. The couple of open minded teachers from the Yeshivah, who I personally chose to write the recommendations, aided the selection process; and finally when the records were turned over.......... She was immediately accepted. The only problem remaining, or so it seemed; was that by the time the records had been turned over, no scholarship money remained for the upcoming academic year.

Here I was a single parent, with three children and a job I knew would now be on shaky grounds, with my daughter's withdrawal; where was I to find twelve thousand dollars? I lost sleep for several days; for although I knew that there was no decision, that Tzipporah needed that school as surely as she required oxygen to breathe, I had no idea how I was going to pay for it. Then the very next night it came to me. Tzipporah had to go to that school. Somehow the tuition would be paid. I had to do it on faith alone; in Hebrew we call it Bitachon, and Bitachon was all I would have to go on. I got up from my unsettled bed. I opened the envelope. I signed the paperwork. I made out the deposit check. I put a stamp on the school addressed envelope; then I laid down my head and slept for the first time in days.

Little did I know that the decision would be nothing compared to the other upsets that would come my way; but it didn't matter. I had signed the paperwork. She was going to that school.

The summer before she would start at her new school would move slowly, I endeavoured to find another job outside of the Yeshivah, living on painfully little, and now trying to make payments on this enormous tuition, in addition to food and rent. In the end, the Yeshivah would call me back to do some nasty job or other that no one else would do. In the end, Holidays gifts and my own school loans would fit the bill; but in between there would be a lot of worry, and a lot of living from hand-to-mouth.

Right after school started, my car breathed its last and we would be carless for months. Fortunately, I had begged my mother for the bonds, she had put away for me, to pay for the school bus to take Tzippi back and forth each day. My mother's eternal 'public school mentality' had always angered her in understanding the financial loses (I saw them as investments) I paid in private schooling my brood.

Tzippi's first school year, at her future alma mater, would prove exciting and demanding. It would take her sometime to come to grips with the social differences, but the academic demands she responded to immediately – IT WAS A FIT!!!

Meanwhile life outside her school continued. In time, our Orthodox Jewish neighborhood became more and more aware of her change in academic venue. These people, who had proved so supportive financially, socially, and in every other way imaginable, all of a sudden made a one hundred eighty degree turn on their axes. I almost had to refocus to recognize them for the 'friends', they had once been. I learned a lot about friends that year. Just as Tzippi, simultaneously, was learning to accept other people from other environments; I was learning the hard facts of which of my friends really were my friends, what unconditional friendship really meant, and the 'sins' or blindness of far right groups. I don't know who proved to learn more that year; but surely both of our lives were changed forever.

I've changed a lot in the way I view both the Orthodox Jewish community and how I view friendship in general. I've distanced myself in many ways from the first and have learned to hold my remaining friends and new friends much dearer, as well as to a new light. There are people I still see from time to time whose eyes always look at me quizzically and judgmentally. Their unspoken words being – how badly did 'the child' turn out. I always answer their unspoken questions audibly and proud – my daughter, Tzippi, is a Ph.D. candidate in Bio-Chem. In addition, states and miles away, she is the one who provides me, her mother, disabled with Multiple Sclerosis, the greatest assistance.

It seems for all my pain; I have had the last laugh.

Each Day Is A Gift

Each day is a gift, G-d.

Each day is a gift.

Each vision we see,

Each scent that we smell,

Each thing that we do,

We're opportuned.

Each day is a gift, G-d.

Each day is a gift.

Going to Bed in Daylight

In closing the window,

I notice that the sky is still blue;

I remember, as a child,

    that my parents forced me to go to bed

    while it was still light.

Now, as an adult,

    circumstances do.

Perhaps there is little difference;

The sadness still remains

    within me.

A House Becomes Us

I've just begun to notice the character that is to be found in the walls that shelter me. It took me a year to be able to do that. The first year living here I was too depressed, too filled with the sense of loss, to notice much of anything. Now, though, I've become more able to look deeper into the characters who share the building with me, and my cat, Suche. Laughter has come easier, as I notice the habits of management, as well as the other tenants who inhabit this space. It doesn't really mean that I've come to like it any better; tolerate it, would seem a better term. Much of it lies, I guess, in dealing with the loss of a much beloved home, existence, and so many items full of so much memory.

Truth be known, there was only one home that I really loved since I left my house of origin; and that was that very last one. It was the only one I would come home to without disgust and depression, the only one I came into completely on my own financial feet. Nor is this the only one I've had the produced such sadness. I remember the two bedroom, three floor walk up, where the children and I spent three years. Filled with all the nasty, gristly items that enable us to label a tenement, a tenement; that house served us in getting us started in a community that was to turn out to be our home in so many ways. We made many friends there and became integral parts of it. So I can now say so what to the roaches and mice, so what to the malfunctioning faucets and toilet, to the nonlocking backdoor........................So What! It was there I would fall in love, albeit ending unhappily. It would be there that my children would make links that would seemingly serve to anchor them for a lifetime............Although   one   would   choose   other shackles...........................

Each house has an inherent personality of its own, and in time, this personality merges with its occupants to produce something completely new; something that will not be replicated when a new inhabitant comes to stay.

When I look back at my many homes, good and bad, I can smile now; much of the pain is gone. Like yellowed photos in a scrap book, they now loom large with the memories I cherish. Recently in my new abode, I find myself daily passing the first home I inhabited as a single adult. It had its own horrors, surely, but now I look at it differently, with increased self respect. How did I survive it all – the neighborhood alone must have been brutal; remembering how I got myself out of there in just under a year, even if it was to reshackle myself for sometime to come.

In one home during that poor marriage, I remember a big house where the previous tenant's unneutered cat had sprayed and permanently scented the entire premises. I remember the nasty owner, who upon hearing my complaint over the poorly working freezer, actually put his finger in my ice cream to test it out; and who would just walk into the house unannounced, as the bell he said worked – didn't................

I remember the lovely garden apartment my daughters were born in – too small but largely inhabitable - the one we should have bought – had my ex-husband not been so parent controlled.

I remember the townhouse – the last place I resided as a married woman – way beyond our finances – a hope and dream for a year and then a scurrying out on my own – a mother hen with a brood of three to care for – and little, if anything, to lean on....................................

Each house sits on various points in my memory cortices. Opening its doors to the dreams I had and dreams left behind. I no longer hate any of them. Like an old lover, one can choose to remember the charismatic parts, the music, the laughter, even if the dream – were there one – has died.

At this point of my life, living truly alone for my first time, all I truly want to do is write and research. This unseemly abode was supposed to be my garret. As luck would have it, garrets proved too expensive that season - so I ended up here - in one which takes too much time to earn its keep.

I spent the first year endeavouring to adapt – the place, the building, the community, the new transport system; nothing worked. Now like a seasoned adversary – I accept it as here – and me as here within it. I reason that it's a limited sentence – and one where I only have to find the way out. In looking for how I have changed it's personality – I look at the simplistic smile faces I embossed the mail box and apartment door on day one or the more sophisticated quotes I hung to grace the wall around my computer desk. And yet, all in all, I find little of me here, I still hate to touch and clean parts of it; and, as I did during the two week stay with my middle child's family as I waited the apartment's readying, I often feel homeless, still.

Growth is never an easy thing. It was often my saddest eras which enabled me to move on – the tremendous depression I would find upon awakening in that cat sprayed house, the feeling of isolation in that first single adult abode's phonelessness, that incidentally cost me a job.

Knowing how being so unhappy on my twenty first birthday could only be a sign of needing to move on or how my father's demise led me to reembrace life. So, these many and varied abodes, each in their own way, has ushered me on – sometimes seemingly up, sometimes otherwise – but always on. In many ways we never truly know if something is better or worse, as human beings, we never truly see the whole picture; but in the snippets I've been allotted – I have seen clear steps. There have been moments of great thanks, times of ecstatic joy. As human beings what more could we ask. And so at this point in my existence, in this most unsatisfactory abode, I know more so, that I just want to write and research – and DAMN the house - I will.

How I Spent My Summer Vacation

As an educator, I remember the principal, of the first school of my employment, starting each school year cautioning the English staff not to assign the traditional 'How I Spent My Summer Vacation' composition to their students. Looking back now, I can see how he was both wrong and right simultaneously. His goal was to start the school year in earnest; the 'Today is the First Day of the Rest of Your Life' message and that was good. On the other hand, summer was a very special time to our students. They were not urban children imprisoned in tenement walls. They were children of affluence or relative affluence. They had seen things, done things, and largely had a good time of it. One could equally ponder - what of the student who had had a miserable time – did she/he not provide the argument the principal may have needed. My gut reaction, is largely not. Classroom teachers, by the very nature of the classroom itself, must teach to the majority; and the decided majority loved to tell of their summertime fun. Alright one may say, that if they had so much fun, can't we go on from here?! Well, yes we can, but should we? To bring a student into the classroom means to bring his/her mind along with her/him. Here we have this magnificent summer story – let's open the door to the children's memories and use them as an opportunity to teach the telling of a good story along the way. I thought of this situation recently when upon autumn's immergence, I reflected on my own summer and the forming of my own story.

In the summer of my fiftieth year, my physical infirmity had gotten to the point of depriving me of the ability to drive and making the use of a walking stick obligatory. In addition, my two year stint at a grubby, seedy customer service company, kept me inside during the week when the long summer sunny days called out to me; not making my already ill fit within the company, itself, any more agreeable. I would arrive each morning just as light was coming to the skies and leave just in time to witness the waning hours of the summer night. Although summer is the longest of the Earth's daylight hours, eleven hour workdays proved to stunt even that. And so it was this summer, knowing that I could neither drive to my beloved seaside, nor afford to take off the time to enjoy the summer sun that I looked at summer – my favourite season - with some dismay and depression. After all, in all one's school training days - one's summers are free - here I was in my fiftieth summer – and free I was not. But as I have often found in some of my most difficult, moments days, and years something occurs –

something miraculous – from nowhere – or perhaps - everywhere appears. The miracle 'happening', to use a 1960's – 70's term, took the form of my youngest daughter.

My youngest daughter, Tzipporah, was always an interesting mixture of traits. As the youngest she should have been the baby and the babiest, reeling in all the goodies that the final child is usually entitled. As luck or life would have it, Tzippi, never was able to bask in the traditional baby role. She had a sister, who due to her own limitations, would prove to fulfill it for her. So in the end, Tzipporah the baby, became Tzipporah the caretaker; and this was the summer where she became mine as well.

When I finally told my children of my long secreted ailment; Tzippi was the only one who really appeared to understand. Perhaps it was her background in Bio-Chemistry, perhaps it was our life long relationship of understanding one another without speaking. Be that as it may, Tzippi, once again, knew what it was that I was in need. That spring in a little wrapped package, Tzippi had given me my summer vacation in the form of my Mother's Day present. I would open up the ribbon and shiny paper to find bus tickets to her off campus home.

It would take me to mid July, but on a wet, gloomy morning I packed my bag; careful not to over pack as now, without my car, I would have to carry and I no longer had the physical resources for that either. I mounted the succession of buses for my trip. It could have been a disagreeable occurrence. The buses were overcrowded, and tightly holding onto my luggage to give others space, did not give much room for even a meagre sized me. And yet it was wonderful. I took in all the sites, sounds, and smells, and would not permit the rain to dampen my spirits. The trip would prove about seven and a half hours, but they flew; and after a day of experiences and memories the bus driver, who up to the moment had given no hint of even being aware of my presence, took my bag, swung open the door, and handing my belongings to my daughter, drove away. We embraced. I was with her. I felt at home.

The weekend would prove to fly, but like my trip there, it would prove to brighten my life with all its vivid pictures and memories. First, making sure that I wasn't ravenous, my youngest daughter, my baby, walked me across campus. I thought at first that we were heading to her car; we were, as it would turn out, heading to the campus hotel. I had presumed that I was spending the weekend in the apartment she shared with friends; she, instead, put me up in this rather expensive visitor's center; footing the bill all by herself, on her rather meagre grad school income.

From there, we would dine on a fabulous Greek salad – the best I have ever had – and explore the campus from which I had heard so much, but never seen. She would take me through the fabulous laboratories and the pastoral settings – equipped with farm animals and an onsite ice cream parlor, behind which the ice cream was actually made from the milk and cream of the very cows I had been fortunate enough to visit. Over the course of an extremely rainy weekend, she would make me feel at home in her apartment, feed me generously, and acquaint me with the whole geographic area, both on and off campus that had become her home. Always knowing my likes and dislikes, she squirreled aside extra time for the viewing of the libraries and bookstore sections. She, even in the pouring rain, knowing my love of duck ponds, brought me to an expansive area where the geese and ducks lived undisturbed by any who would mean them harm. All along, she quietly assured my physical comfort and that all my needs were met. She painted my nails, knowing that they hadn't been touched for so very long. She found me a good movie, a challenging board game, and in the end helped me board the bus homeward.

The buses back were overcrowded and not very timely, but it didn't matter. My daughter's gift – my Mother's Day present – was all that mattered. In those brief few hours, between Friday's bus boarding and Sunday's return, I had had my summer vacation. Compared to some of the summers of the affluent children with whom I once worked, it would have seemed inexpensive and slight; but in reality, had my daughter given me both sun and moon, it couldn't have meant more.

I Survived Another Winter

I survived another winter

And it's been a long, long drag;

I survived another winter

As if in G-d's own plan;

I survived another winter

And I've begun the springing thaw;

I survived another winter

And I'm asking G-d for more.

An Immigrant Nation

I'm afraid that we're going to have to send our beloved Lady Liberty back to France. We can honestly hold onto her no longer. Instead of protecting those "huddled masses yearning to be free", we now send them back en masse, sometimes to face death or disfigurement, such as in dictatorial nations or in women circumcising Africa. Once we may have been that "lamp beside the golden door", now we're merely the golden trap, enticing, imprisoning, and turning away. The Statute of Liberty was always the view most desired by ocean traveling immigrants. Sick, hungry, impoverished, and frightened, they came to these shores with only the hopes of freedom. Having now barred this singular wish, it is time to remove the advertisement, that one hundred fifty-one foot billboard.

Life was never easy for immigrants in this country; and indeed it could be well said that immigration is not easy in any country. Yet historically, our country's fathers did design us as a nation of immigrants. The pilgrims came to Plymouth Rock; approximately one hundred men from the London Company came to Jamestown. They were different populations and yet they came to be free. Some flourished, some starved, some may have even wished to return; but all and all, our nation's Declaration of Independence, Constitution, and Bill of Rights were all written on their backs, due to their American and immigrant experiences. This is not to paint America as the land of golden sidewalks. We were not perfect then, nor are we perfect now.

Nor is this the first era of immigrant bigotry. Indeed each cycle of immigrants brought its own seething hate. Regardless of geographic, ethnicity, or religious origin, immigrants were historically met with widespread fear and ostracism. The Chinese were hated for their physical appearance, and even hurt one another; with existing Chinese business owners making indentured slaves out of their Chinese brethren. And yet these peoples, by and large, came in and enriched themselves and the United States as a whole. The Jews, too, were not greeted lovingly, and while they worked hard and prospered there were quotas greeting them on University doors; law firms, country clubs, closed communities, and entire professions very clearly said 'Stay Out'. The Irish, although religious Christians, were greeted with no greater love; although they too responded by becoming part and parcel of society. Indeed, they became our police force.

Nor was the current problem of immigrant criminality new. Indeed any number of Jamestown Colony members were just that; buying their freedom by sailing to these shores and labouring. Obviously some waves of immigrants have brought more culturally to our country than others. It would be as big a lie to ignore that fact as to ignore our current immigrant mistreatment. Yet all and all, Lady Liberty does not state only the fair haired, intelligent, hardworking, wealthy, or gifted may apply. Instead her torch welcomed the "homeless", the "wretched".

Perhaps when we closed her doors out of fear of terrorism, we made a large mistake. Lady Liberty certainly did not pat the humble immigrant down for weapons. Surely immigrants were always eyed with suspicion and fear. All living beings possess a sense of danger of the new and unknown as protection mechanisms; that's basic biology. But biology needn't keep away the needy. History has not shown the bulk of those seeking asylum to be harmful. Our current 'Big Brother' policies can't rewrite two hundred some odd years of immigration history.

Does this mean that we 'must take' everyone who seeks entry at our shores? Possibly. Why does this scare the American public so? If you're educated and in a highly demanding profession, the immigrant is highly unlikely to be competing for your position, house, or beach cabana any too soon. If you're of less affluence, well, you live in the wealthiest nation in the world - get some training and go out and better yourself and your family. Our restaurants throw out unbearable amounts of food. No one need starve here. F.D.R.'s administration showed how in putting a broom and very basics items in the unemployed hands, we could have the population working and improving American life.

If your concern is the overcrowding of schools and hospitals, think instead of the employment of builders to build more schools and hospitals, of teachers and medical staff to service them, and of the businesses to buy supplies from. This all spells economic movement; growth, where there had been stagnation.

For those fearing the price tag on reviving our nation's economy, our nation's soul, look instead at the money we spend killing people all over the world, at the money we spend hunting down immigrants and keeping them out. Perhaps there are better, more humanitarian programs, we can harness with the American dollar; perhaps they can start with these very same immigrants.

Our Beloved Lady, herself was an immigrant, a gift from France to the United States. Built on the appreciation of America's living out of the European Enlightenment. Each time we accepted a ship load of those "huddled masses" we earned her; each time we sent a boat back, we shunned her.

Elementary school teachers frequently assign a self revelation project to students, where the students have to go back home to their parents and families, at large, to enquire into their ethnic roots. This is the U.S.A. assignment peculiar to us, as we are all immigrants; indeed, if you are not a pure blooded Native American, you are an immigrant by virtue of your parentage.

Obviously immigration is no panacea. This is true for those coming here as well as for those of us already in residence, but since when is perfection expected. The leaders who wrote the Declaration of Independence, the Constitution, and the Bill of Rights, were not expecting heaven on earth. The events leading to their publication were certainly nothing like heaven. Our Lady certainly was not conceived in a perfect world view either; and she's required much upkeep and money to keep her shining the immigrants' way. Whether we like it or not, by virtue of our birth here, we are part and parcel of the immigrant experience. If we were born here we're merely lucky; but why should our personal fortune keep others out?

It's Not Politically Correct

You're going to say that I'm prejudiced and that's fine. If this gets even one person thinking then it's working. If my raising of thought gets people's danders up; so be it. In the Middle Ages, people had to wait to the middle of the night to raid graves to experiment and study the dead, because experimenting on the dead made people and the Church angry. Copernicus made the Church so angry that they put him to death for his study and teachings.   Jesus   fared   little better..............................

I grew up during the Civil Rights Era. It was an exciting and important time to live in and I, for one, championed it. Jews and blacks marched together for the rights of all people. Soon women, too, would burn their brassieres, and demand equal time, rights, and speech.................................That was all good and meaningful, but where has it led us today??????????????????

I work with any number of uneducated Afro-Americans and Hispanics. They are largely angry and bitter. They will gladly tell you, whether you ask or not, how unfair everything is in this country for minorities. I grew up championing this belief; but something rings wrong here. Since my childhood years, many advances were made in Civil Rights. We have all sorts of equal opportunity, housing, employment, and special education acts that in some cases bend over backwards for just such minorities. This isn't to say it's easy to be a minority. The fact is, it's not easy to be any human being. Living is a challenge. Growing up is a challenge. Working is a challenge. Bringing up a family is a challenge. However, these are not the only minorities in the U.S.A.. My brother-in-law is a first generation Chinese-American. His family came here before he was born. They ALL worked very hard. His father died very young. My brother-in-law worked very hard, too. He went to Yale. He entered and won any number of international architectural contests. He's a highly successful architect with a wife and a child.

My father was born within the first decade of the twentieth century. He wanted to become an engineer, but he was simply told that Jews couldn't become engineers; so he became an attorney. He entered law school back when there were still quotas. He finished seventh in his class.

There are also plenty of Afro-American and Hispanics who have worked hard and succeeded. I think of a friend of mine. She has an M.B.A.. No one handed that to her. She runs her interactive theatre company where she teaches industry how to deal with diversity and currently is running a social program dealing with preventing teenage pregnancies and abusive relationships.

Life is hard, but it's that much harder if you're without a compass, goals, or role models. But you have to begin somewhere.

Last summer several minority young people were murdered right before leaving for college. Their parents complained that these children had studied and done everything that was right and look what happened to them. Look, indeed. The children may well have been on the right road, but their parents owed them protection. Why the hell didn't they get them out of a dangerous area. Yes, I know things are expensive. So work two jobs, don't buy everything that glitters, save your money and move somewhere SAFE!!!!!!!!!!!!!!!!!!!!!!!!!!

I watch these employees every day. When they're given educational opportunities, they don't complete them. When they're given jobs, they don't show up on time, and are frequently out. When the least little thing goes wrong, they up and quit. People who want to get ahead don't behave that way. They tough it out. They stay in school. They work hard and get better and better jobs. And they don't buy every shiny bauble they see on payday....................

Successful minorities need to teach those who are lost. And the message must be clear. First you start with girls, because statistics show that more female minorities have succeeded than their male counterparts. You teach them to stay in school and not to sleep with everything in sight. Teach them the dangers of early sexual experimentation and teenage pregnancy. Preach against illegitimacy. Teach these girls to like themselves enough to become something.

If the girls are not lying around waiting for these clueless minority males, perhaps they too will see the light. If these young women educate themselves, they won't want to be linked with uneducated and unemployed men. The males will have to work a lot harder to become something, themselves, when the women refuse to have promiscuous relations and demand marriage, a house, and a monogamous life style.

Girls who are reading books to make something of themselves, will one day be teaching their children to do the same by way of example. They're our only future, our only chance. It's a hard message to teach, but until minority leaders preach it – no one will

listen……………………………………..

Leaves of Life

Much like the leaves

When we're young

We're green and beautiful

As we age

We become colourful and exciting

Then we grow brown and still.

Letter to My Employer

Dear Boss,

There's a wonderful, new change in my life. I've given birth to a baby, but I want to be the first to assure you that there will be no change in my work. In just six weeks I will be back in the office again. Of course, now instead of working 8:00 am to 5:00 pm, plus overtime, I will be working 6:00 pm to 8:00 pm with no overtime. True, this change of hours arithmetically proves to be a thirty-five hour per week reduction; however, in reality you will find it is anything but. I will actually be giving you a greater time period. I will be giving you my quality time. Surely my quality time is worth at least double of my former hours; which is why I will also be requesting a raise. That is, once I'm back at work. Now, while it is true that you will not be able to call or disturb during my original hours, after all, I will be busy with my new baby; however, once I'm there – I'm there, barring, of course unforeseeable emergencies or convergences, but there's no need to worry about that now.

So, see you in six weeks.

Yours truly,

Your Employee

Surely, you're laughing by now, perhaps deep within a nearly convulsive laugh rage. But why? Why is this so funny? Because no employer in his/her right mind would accept this. Thirty-five hours per week hour reduction and a raise, to boot? Yet, all across America women are doing just that. Oh, no, we're not writing absurd job/career destroying letters; we're doing something far worse. We're writing these letters to our children.

We give birth to a beautiful baby - the baby of our dreams. We stay home wallowing in nothing but baby, baby, baby for six weeks' time and then we don a suit and pick up this completely helpless individual and drop him or her off in a daycare center, where, if we're educated and highly intelligent, the staff, now bringing up the child of our dreams, is likely to have two thirds to three quarter of our IQs. The care takers may barely even speak English.

Now, I must apologize to those women out there whose families, without their wife or mother's full time wages, will have neither food to eat, nor a roof to sleep under, nor clothes to wear. We're women and we do what we have to do, but this employee's letter is not about 'doing what we have to do'; it's about trying to have 'it all'! Well, ladies, I'm sorry, NO ONE CAN HAVE IT ALL!!!! If you want to save that seven layer chocolate layer cake for tomorrow; you can't eat it now. If you want to wear that bikini tomorrow; you can't have the cake either. If you want to be a career woman giving your all for the work world; then you can't give your all for the baby, too. No matter how you slice it, there are only so many hours in the day – a little less than twenty-four - to be scientifically correct, I'm told. Were you even to largely give up sleep, how would you arrange it; work at night while your baby slept and raise the baby during the day while your body craves sleep? I know women who have tried; it takes its toll. In the end neither work, nor the baby, nor the job wins and what you've done to your mind and body may not be repairable.

Recently I heard a young career woman, wife, and mother complain that no one had warned her how her career would suffer once she had a baby. One wonders if she was warned how the baby might suffer once she resumed her job?

I had the added benefit and sad responsibility in dealing with preschoolers of largely working mothers. These were largely children of affluence. Their mothers weren't putting hamburger on the table; they were adding digits to the family's investment income, purchasing McMansions, large expensive vehicles, and embarrassingly expensive vacations. Is this a sin? No, and I'm not here to judge. I'm merely sharing my years of experience with children, my own and many others and asking women and society at large to begin to think about what all this really means, not just to our finances, but to our future generations.

I remember very early in my pre-school work world, dealing with a very sad little girl. She was a beautiful child of Middle Eastern heritage. Dark skin, dark, bright eyes, and long black hair. Two recollections come to mind when I think of her. The first was in conducting a Thanksgiving group lesson, each child was asked to list one thing he or she was thankful for. In lieu of answers of a new baby brother, a parent, a nice house, a great grandparent, that I was hearing elsewhere; this little girl's response was a nice babysitter. But the evidence was not to end there. One day the child came down with some childhood malady. Taken to the office, she was found to have a high fever. The secretary speedily called the child's mother at work. The mother instructed the woman to call the father. The father, once called, instructed the secretary to call the mother. I don't remember which parent finally showed up, but I do remember that it was three hours later.

Unfortunately this is not the rare blimp on the screen. I remember one Pre-School Professional, who speedily whisked her son off to speech therapy. She mentioned to me that she had no idea why he spoke the way he did. I asked her if the child's caretaker had been Jamaican; she said yes and inquired as to how I knew. His speech patterns, I explained to this 'Pre-School' expert, were Jamaican.

One sweet little boy came into school each morning half asleep. Finally the parents, who took turns dropping the child off; but always ran out as fast as they could, were told of our concern of the child's continual weariness. A half amused, half sheepish smile appeared on the father's face. You see, he told us, we both have very long hours and get home quite late; but we must have that quality time with our children. Quality time, in this particular family, translated to keeping their very young children up an hour to an hour and a half each night past what would be considered an average bedtime. One might wonder what this quality time was designed for and for whom it proved to be qualitative.

The anecdotals my colleagues and I have shared for years are endless. They are not limited to certain geographic zones, types of schools, or age or gender. What our experience held in common, was what occurred to children in families where they were largely separated from their parents for most of their waking hours. We saw academic, behavioral, and social lacks. We also saw families who seemed largely to have forgotten what family life was about; families' whose values seemed to have been outside their children's interests.

Once again, I am not a judge. I'm merely a middle aged mother and former educator/counselor who would like to get society thinking. When I was raising my, now grown children, I was largely a single mother; and yet I fought to be with them, ending up working in their schools for less than adequate pay or benefits, albeit, to be with them watching and helping them grow. They were my life, my ultimate pleasure, and responsibility. I chose to have them and I've never been sorry.

If you're thinking about having children today you have more choices than anyone ever imagined; but one that few people mention is that of opting not to have children at all. There is no physiological reason to have a child today if you don't want to. Children are not a part time job. They do not give holidays or vacations off. They take at least two decades to raise and there is always that chance, no matter what the laboratory tests and doctors tell you, that a child may need a caretaker for a lifetime. If you don't want to do this; why do it? Why have children? If you need Christmas cards pictures, you can hire a child from a modeling agency; whatever the cost is it will be far less than childraising. You don't have to bear children to endow your parents with grandchildren; there are plenty of children out there who would gladly adopt a grandparent for a few hours every week or month. If you grew up with this picture of the perfect size family – then rethink it – perfect only exists in pictures (and then that too is questionable). A family – that is children - means work. This is work that never takes a day off and never goes away. No matter who you hire or what you do to avoid it, children get sick or hurt or require you in an instant. No matter what you want or need to do, they need you then. If you don't want that kind of responsibility; that's fine. You don't have to. You wouldn't adopt puppy if you couldn't handle paper training; why would you chose to have a child if you didn't want to handle the commitment.

Finally, for those of you out there who would like to do both; here's my suggestions. If you choose to have your children early, you will have lots of energy for them – perhaps not as much patience though- and then later, if all goes well, you can start a career. If instead, you choose to have children later, you'll have less energy (probably more money) but much more patience and probably a better idea of what's truly important, as you've seen the realities of that not so perfect work world. Either way, children are the greatest gift only when you're able to receive them into the kind of commitment they require to thrive and so deserve.

Letter To My Youngest Child

Dear Tzippi,

As I watched you across the table in the restaurant the other night I couldn't stop shaking my head in amazement. Where had the time gone? Wasn't it just yesterday that you were entering high school. Weren't we only just planning your Bat Mitzvah celebration? Weren't you only just going away to sleepaway camp for the very first time? I don't know. But it surely seems that way.

And yet now - then - sitting there looking at you on the eve of your eighteenth year. I think of all the special hours, days, and moments that are behind us. All those Kodak Moments which make up a childhood. And yet there you are, a whole person. A young adult. A full human being - never to be a real child - a real little girl again.

Of course the eighteenth year - your eighteenth birthday is surely a rite of passage - something we in the psych world make a big deal over. But this rite of passage isn't only for you - but me as well. As you're taking these big steps - leaving home - packing for college - I too am taking steps. I, too, am moving on. Just yesterday - or so it seems - we were just starting out together - pregnancy - birth - infancy - toddlerhood. Taking one giant step at a time TOGETHER. Now, we will continue taking these steps - steps which move us through life, but these steps will be largely APART.

What then can I wish you? How then can I instruct you - help you - aid you as you enter this adulthood of self propelled steps? There are no easy answers. In many ways you were always self propelled - always knowing who you were - and where you wanted to be. However, I was always there, watching and forming that parently cushion - parachute - if you will - for you to fallback upon. I will still be here - of course - for as long as I live - and spiritually ever after; and yet your decisions will be your own. Do I worry about these decisions - largely not . You really are mature beyond your years and always have been. And yet, I worry about my sensitive daughter and the unkind world - I worry about my workaholic and the potential slave. And yet I know how capable you are and how extremely intelligent, creative, and insightful you are. Indeed in many ways I envy all those who will watch you in action in this your new adult existence. After all, I feel so fortunate to have been spoiled to have had experienced your growth through maturity.

What then, you may ask, do I have to offer you - on this your passage into 'grownuphood'? Several points of wisdom - if you will - that have kept me going throughout the years. One is always be yourself - this way regardless of the results you never feel cheated - things might not have worked out as you had hoped - but you remained true to you. Two is don't be afraid to walk - or even run - away - if it feels wrong - it probably is. And three is don't be afraid to pursue your dreams - they may seem far or even impossible at times, but they are out there - for you to reach for and find. They make take much work, much trial and error, much disappointment; but if you always reach for your dreams, they will come true.

Lastly, just because you're leaving me - that doesn't mean I'm leaving you. I will always be here to help pick up the pieces or even to celebrate - call - write - e-mail.

I LOVE YOU VERY MUCH,

MAAAAAAAAAAAAAAAA

Letting Go

One of the by parts or side effects, beneficial or otherwise, that my Multiple Sclerosis has given me, is the ability to let go. This of course could be found even earlier in my life, with my greater and greater acceptance of the Creator; but it has become that much more so, as the M.S. progresses. For while, I was never a materialist, I was always perseverant; this indeed was the personality trait that kept me fighting for all the things my children needed. My mother would say that there would be "no way" someone in my financial class could provide my children with sleepaway camp or orthodontics, or private school; and yet I did so, year after year. That single minded hard headedness, kept me working in places I hated, living in places I'd rather not, and associating with those I'd rather have nothing to do. It, no doubt, cost me much in health, happiness, and general well being; but nonetheless it, by and large, met my goal as a parent. I did the impossible.

There is a saying, I'm yet to trace to its origin, known well in the not-for-profit world, which goes as follows:

Those of us,

Who have done so much,

For so long,

With so little;

Now think,

We can do anything,

With nothing at all!

Just as that may well have been the credo of the many organizations of which I was a part, it had, doubtlessly, become my theme song, as well. Indeed I remember nights when there was little remaining of the food funds for the pay period. I would look through the refrigerator and pantry; and night after night, somehow, meals would appear and my children never went hungry. I would take eggs and frozen vegetables and make fancy soufflés. In fact, my earlier gourmet cooking skills enabled me to make that something from 'nothing at all'. Nonetheless, such strivings take their toll.

My children, now grown, two with children of their own to feed, no longer make the same demands on me. In fact, the demands upon my life are new, in many ways, to a person who never really lived on her own until now. Having gone from home of origin, to early marriage, to single parenthood; being alone, to say nothing of my feline companion, is still largely new to me. And yet the perseverance persevered. But so did the M.S..

I'm noting more and more, that sometimes at the highest point, the apex, of the worry, that I come to think that something good must come of this. I do what I can, but in many cases, I find myself letting go. Certainly that must be a kinder response to my mind and body. Certainly that must leave my body and mind less susceptible to the M.S.; and yet I still find myself going back and forth on the notion. In some ways, part of myself just acquiesces, after so many years; and just lets go. At times, I see it as a good omen in dealing with the many things that lie ahead that as the Serenity Prayer guides us:

G-d grant me the serenity

To accept the things I cannot change

The courage to change the things I can

And the wisdom to know the difference.

But letting go creates a philosophical argument in my head, if you will. My mother, and the many other nonreligion forces in my background, spoke of the Opium of Catholicism or Organized Religion; of course there was a certain truth to that. However, the Communist world created its own Opium, if you will, in the G-dless state. The Deity became the state; and its leaders, and the Opium, no less potent. Personally I would far prefer to rely on G-d than any man or any state, or woman, for that matter.

Letting go, also, brings to mind the fears created by the progression of the M.S., where I fear others making decisions for me; not only the medical profession, whom I loathe, but my family. That I took the preventative stand of naming my youngest daughter as power-of-attorney, knowing full well that she was the only one who would understand my needs, beliefs and desirers, should I be unable to speak for myself.

In the end, letting go may foster my entire entity as a human being, the serenity the prayers speaks of; allowing my limited energies to work on those things I am able to do or to those things I prefer to channel them. Letting go may not be the perfect system, not the prefect answer for everything or everyone; however, this is not a perfect world. In each situation, in each decision, on each day, hour, and moment, decisions are forced upon us. Sometimes there is nothing or little we can or choose to do. Sometimes we are lost to the 'correct' response. Sometimes we can only let go.

The Lie Called Equality

They've sat in front of me year after year, the parents, the children, all whining with the same mistaken notion. It's not fair, they would tell me. My brother gets As without even trying; and I study all night, only to achieve Bs. My neighbor has a much nicer bike then mine; and she never does anything around her house. My children are never satisfied with anything I do; if I give everyone chocolate cake, someone always complains that his/her piece is smaller or not as nice. Of course the complainers are immediately put off by my all too evident demeanor; you see, I've heard it all too often before. You're right it's not fair, I would go on to tell them - nothing really is....

For years I would have this instructional dialogue with parents in this never ending discussion of fairness. I would say look at the mother with five children, if Brian needs braces, must all the other four children get braces as well? The elicited answer of no is always received. Good, I'd say. Now, if in this same family of five, Albert deliberately brakes the livingroom window, must all the other four children get spanked as well? The elicited response is a little more nervous this time, but it comes – no – I'm told. Well, the other four children were treated fairly according to these scenarios but does that make all of life's dealings equitable? Of course not.

From the time a child watches his brother receive the chocolate cake first and all the way through elementary school, secondary schools, and college, the growing individual is still heard to murmur loudly about the various inequitable situations she/he encounters. These situations end not at graduation, but continue on in the workforce, marriage, business, and the community. The once small child desirous of the chocolate cake, now merely has his/her eye on some other delectable person, position, or item. But this time Mommy isn't there, in all probability, to slice another piece of cake. The now adult individual may choose to proceed to a union organizer, attorney, counselor, arbitrator, etc., etc; but interestingly enough just as that piece of cake was never large enough or good enough, neither will the results of any of these individuals prove better. The point is not that our eyes all always bigger than our stomachs; although they well may be. The point is that the situation really isn't fair. It really isn't equitable and it's conceivably never going to become so.

One could find sources for the right of quality of life for all human beings back to the time of the Greeks, if not further; but in the United States it's easier to start with the Declaration of Independence, where we are informed that "All men are created equal." From these five little words, to say nothing of the European Enlightenment Philosophy from which it derived, we have been fooling ourselves for over two hundred years. Oh, surely it could be argued that the Declaration itself and our nation's fathers were the ones portraying this fallacy, but that would not be completely accurate. For one thing, these forefathers also gave the nation the Electoral College; so obviously the feeling was that we weren't all equal in our skills of choice making. In addition, both slaves and women's supposed rights were ignored by this Declaration, obviously we weren't all considered equal in that light either. But the fallacy symptoms don't end there, poverty immediately showed up as a de-equalizer when the role of president insisted on landowning. And indeed the tally has only begun.

When two individuals go to court and one is wealthy and one is not, the one with the better educated and more experienced attorney, namely the wealthier of the two, will certainly have the edge. When a single individual sues a corporation or government agency, once again, the clout and finances of the larger body is certainly going to outweigh those of the individual. The equity of the legal system, of which so much is supposedly based in a Democratic society, is as much to blame as the popular view of it. We are instructed, ad nauseum, in the United States, both in the school system as well as within the very governmental agencies themselves, of the assuredness of this equality, but it is a falsehood at best. A child in court is not treated equally, the child, if necessary, will be assigned an appropriate guardian; whatever that may be, but he or she will not be treated as an equal to the adult in the suit. This will be also the case for an individual deemed of less than average intelligence or mental understanding. Once again the argument might be that the fairness here lies in the courts' protection of these individuals; and while that may or may not prove to be the case, in the long run it is not equality, as already the individual is deemed less than a full equal.

Of course the government cannot be blamed in toto for this equality lacking society, because equality cannot be found in nature or the society at large either. Two babies are born. One baby is born full term, the other six weeks early; what are the odds of equality here? Okay, we'll blame nature for a while. Now let's take a look at two other babies. Two babies are born. Both infants are six weeks premature. One child is born at an under equipped city hospital; the other is born at an up to date university medical center. What are the chances here?

Well, here we can blame society. Of course some would take the argument a step further, two babies are born in the up to date university medical center. Both children are watched carefully and after a very lengthy stay get to go home to their families. Both children are offspring of poor inner city families; but Charlie's family is poor and loving and Charlie blooms under the love and watchful eye of his parents, grandparents, aunts, uncles, sisters and brothers. Jimmy, the other baby, goes home to his family, too; but Jimmy's father is abusive and one night, during a violent interaction with the child's mother and older brother, Jimmy's father strangles Jimmy. So much for the seeming equality of the hospital scene.

Of course a lot of the talk of equality has been historically pointed at the school system. Anne Marie and Mary Jane both grew up in the same town. At age five, Ann Marie is enrolled in the kindergarten of the local public school. Mary Jane is enrolled in the kindergarten of a small private school in a distant town. Once again the question of odds of equality come into question. Some would even have the reader question the rights of Mary Jane to have a private rather than public school education, and correlatily that Anne Marie should be kept out of private school due to lack of parental funds. The equality waters become muddied still further, if the question of equality occurs when the the parents, of the child attending public school, do not believing in private schooling.

The school side of equality, however, ends not in kindergarten, nor with public versus private school attendance. When the requirements and abilities of students become the point of contention, equality rears it's ugly head as rarely before. Josephine is a second grade student in Wilson Elementary School. Jospehine is a B student. She comes to school well groomed, makes friends easily, and is well like by her teachers. Irene is also a second grade student at Wilson. She, also, is earning a B average in her classwork, but Irene comes to school unkempt almost all of the time. She argues with almost all of the other children and has been known to raise her hands to nearly everyone, including her teacher. Irene's mother and caseworker claim that if Irene were earning As that she would be much happier, that the grooming and argumentativness and physical inappropriateness would all vanish; Irene's mother insists that the school system must hire and pay a full time tutor for Irene. Is this situation equitable for Josephine? Should Josephine start coming to school with unmatched socks, missing buttons, and should she hit the child in front of her upon arrival? Irene's case is not as wild as it may seem. There is currently a war raging as far as the equality of special education status and classes. Parents of many a classified child, nowadays, are very likely to demand that he/she be put into a mainstream class even if the child cannot do the work, even if the child causes social and staffing problems, and even if additional costs are incurred to permit this. The argument would be made that the handicapped child has the unalienable right to be treated just like any other student, but is this really so? Let's see. If the class is heterogeneously grouped, this might be so; that would mean that children of mixed abilities, as well as disabilities, would be all grouped together. What then would occur were the class to be instead homogeneously grouped. Let's say this fourth grade class is a gifted class. Only children placing in the top ten percent of their standardized test scores or with psychological testing would be assigned. What happens with equality now? Does a child with severe physical and intellectual disabilities belong in this classroom merely because his parents, attorney, and caseworker deem it fair? What if the testing psychologist concluded that the child could not handle the work involved, would it still be equitable? Let's take a look at a nonhandicapped child, little Micellelynn in another of the school's fourth grades. She only scored on the thirtieth percentile, but her parents insist she belongs there. The school psychologist tests the child and concludes that she has neither the focus nor the ability for this highly academic program. Is this equitable?

Stan Brown went to a top university and finished Summa Cum Laude. He accepted a supposedly challenging position in a large corporation. After several years in the same role, Mr. Brown proceeds to interrogate the human resources manager as to why he hasn't been moved up the ladder. Mr. Brown is gently assured that there simply were no openings. Mr. Brown, being no one's fool, decides to do a little underground networking. He finds out, much to his dismay, that seven people on his level were all promoted during his time there. He also finds out, that four were family members of certain staff members, one was the girlfriend of a human resource staff member, and two were minorities. Mr. Brown is white, Anglo-Saxon, and Protestant. Mr. Brown chooses to confront the human resource manager. The administrator merely informs Mr. Brown that if he doesn't like working for the corporation, that he should leave. No one would argue about the equality of the situation at hand, but it is nevertheless business as usual; and most individuals would not want to go through their entire work careers suing their way to the top, were it even feasible.

Up to now we have been focusing in on the human side of the equality question, but humans are hardly the only living beings on the earth or in this United States of America, which we have been so carefully reviewing. If one dares to look for equality in nature, one is immediately met with the inability to find it there as well. Whether one walks in an untended forest or the carefully kept flowerbeds of a hothouse, one sees flowers of different heights, brilliance, resiliency, and longevity. If one visits the birds of the wild, there will be crows that are stronger, larger, and better able to feed themselves and their families. If one visits the best of zoos or kennels or other wildlife protection programs, one will view animal babies who don't make it versus others born under the seemingly same circumstances who bloom and grow. Is nature equitable? Can we take her/him to court? Would we be able to obtain equal representation against this powerful body if we did; and if we did win, what would we have proven?

A lot of poets, philosophers, legislators, lawyers, and other well meaning individuals, have written tomes regarding equality over the ages. Many of these before the birth of the United States and many since. Most, no doubt, did so with only the best of intentions in their hearts; though there were some, no doubt, who took the occasion to put themselves in a better position, somehow, through their computer or pen. Few reading these words today, would argue against the beauty and sound and aroma of equality for us all. The problem is not with the idea or ideal; the problem is with the reality. We have seen that in reality, equality simply doesn't exist. Matt Jones will simply never be 6'11" when at twenty-one years of age he has grown to his adult height of 5'9".

Jennifer Simms, born with a degenerative eye disease, is unlikely to become a pilot. Max Welsh, a homeless man from Arizona, is unlikely to become president, even if we change the constitution insisting on property holding for presidential eligibility. For the last two hundred plus years, legislators, attorneys, civil rights organizers, teachers, laymen, and spiritual leaders have endeavoured to make our country equitable; they failed, but not from want of a good fight. In accepting the inevitability of their dilemma, where does that leave the otherwise ethical and caring human beings that inhabit this country, that inhabit the entire earth? If equality is unrealistic, how do we insure what is best for ourselves, our children, and one another? We can only do as we have all along, by fighting for the poor, the hurt, the uneducated, by legislating to make the world the best place it can be, by helping one another in anyway we can. The only difference in our fight, in our work, in our perceptions, is that the ends will not be anticipated as equitable; they will only be the best that we humans can insure in our imperfect existence here on earth.

Middleaged Change

Much like that automotive care manual, that sits in the glove compartment, at least when all goes well; we spend our lives in expectation of guidebooks to help us along the way. When you're expecting, you read everything about pregnancy, labor, delivery, and even more about the impending little one. When you take on a new field of study or career, you reach for the stacks, or the net, for everything ever printed. Each life change, be it big or small, can be researched in print or in technology. Changing homes, new marital status, big promotion or conversely job loss, all such issues will find corresponding life maps to take you step by step along the way. And yet there are points of your life where there is apparently no cartography to get you on your way.

The first may well be when you, as a small child, enter a nonparental arena - be it day care, preschool, or nannyhood. Too young to read, you may well be thrust into a world where everything you've learned, up to the present, is topsy-turvy and appears not likely to be the same again. Of course, today, there's tons of pre-school literature devoted to the pre-school set; and yet not for those who are still too young to read it.

The second, may occur many years later, after first jobs, schools, marriages, and childrearing have been navigated, partly by the literary guideposts, and partly by commonsense, intuition, and networking. I feel I have come to that intersection. For a long time now, I am firmly aware that I am not the person I was ten years ago or even five years ago. Of course we are always growing, expanding and changing; but this is a far greater change, much like adolescence or young adulthood. Much though is written about those changes – some we were ready to read – others not so – and yet nonetheless, the guideposts were there – somewhere……………….. In this new era – this era of middle age, I am still looking for my maintenance manual, where's my AAA Card, where's the tow truck if I break down, and where are my peers on this trip?

Last year, after seventeen years of misery, I left my full time position; much to the shock of just about everyone. I had already left the community, where I had spent almost as many years previously. During the last eight and a half months, I have applied for research grants, done temporary work, and even been fired by an employer who thought I was a of a different national origin. In many ways, when I am not concerned about financial issues, I feel I'm more me today than I have been for decades, and yet ofttimes, I feel very much alone.

What shocks me most, is how much on my own plane I feel. Tonight an old friend called me. Before my move and job change, she and I had been inseparable, having gotten each other through many trying situations. Yet tonight, the voice on the phone sounded more the echoes of a stranger, than a woman I once felt closer to than many of my blood relatives. What had changed? Certainly much more than my town of dwelling and profession. What had changed was me....................I wasn't the person whom she had loved and who had loved her. The people and events to which she referred, were all of another time and indeed another life – mine – but not my current life – my former one. Her voice, which once felt like home, only left me wistful and bored. The issues she raised, were no longer my issues. Our gang was no longer my gang, and although she was not a lover but a friend, the love was gone. I remember outgrowing friends in adolescence and late childhood, and I remember watching my own children do the same; but because memory is kind in so many ways, what I didn't remember was the pain.

In my search for a new life, I had become aware I was finally ready for a new mate. Feeling stronger and more stable, I felt the time had finally come; but the stumbling block came as a big surprise. No, it wasn't my persistent shyness or even my lack of physically inviting attributes, but rather it was in my description – I lacked the traits needed to describe who and what I was. Just as I had grown beyond my former job, community, and friends, I had also grown beyond my former personal titles. Indeed who and what am I today? I had grown so fast, I had left my titles behind.

Just as I had to revise my resume dramatically, as I reluctantly search for a position while in actual pursuit of a research grant; I find I now need a resume to describe me/myself as well. For my professional resume, I went to a leader in the field. For help with my grant search, I searched the web for ideas and network. But how does a forty-nine year old woman, who's raised three children alone, risen to a certain level of professional growth, and left a whole developed world behind, describe herself? Middle aged adult in the making?!!

What category do I look under? Where do I fit as I reshape and grow? As one grows and strives in adolescence and young adulthood, one tends not to wonder if one is growing too fast to tie down to one individual or another; but age and maturity changes all that. I've watched married life become a nightmare. I've seen a career as a prison and I've seen a communal life style as intellectual suffocation. In my search for a better life, I'm in search of life quality not quantity.

As a young adult, looking towards marriage and career, one pictures a lifetime ahead. In middle age, one knows how fast that lifetime goes. We've lost family members, friends, and precious time. We know there are no promises, no contractual lifetime agreements; and we accept that grudgingly with the hope of better quality. I leave it to my children, to sign on the line for the thirty year mortgages and IRAs. I have to live for now.

Living for now has cost me sizably financially. My lifelong single sister, in her corporate world, recently scolded me – "Take anything – Anything just so you can have insurance".

Well, I took anything – bad treatment, absurd hours, and even more absurd demands for seventeen years; those days were over. And what kind of insurance? Insurance against what and how and why? No, I was trying not to make the same mistakes that I had made in my well meaning youth.

In many ways, one of my greatest losses, is my former network of friends. Oh, they're still out there. They call me. They send cards. They offer to get together; but it's as if they've come to speak a different language or at least dialect. And so I'm left alone. Happily on my own plane, but with no one save my own children – who fortunately have lives of their own – to share it with. There's no one to share the new insights and victories; and no one to help me through the losses, fears, and pains.

I realize that regardless of the financial outcome, that I was right to make the moves I did. I am glad, in the quiet moments, to know who I am. But when the losses pile up, the fear can hit; and there's no one else who can share or understand it. Part of being an adult, is always knowing, deep inside, that the buck stops here. In some ways it's a comforting truth; for when the buck ends here – the decisions do as well. There are no arguments – it's just me doing the best I can with what I have. In other ways it's knowing that when the last straw comes around, that there will be no one else to pick it up, save for you.

As a highly spiritual individual and eternal optimist, I know that if I can only hold out long enough - that success – whatever that will mean for me – will surely come. A spiritual advisor, from my earlier lifetime, once asked his congregation, that if he could promise them that they would get through the year – would they be alright..... My answer then and now are the same – yes. We need as human beings, to know that we will make 'it' – whatever 'it' is. With that knowledge, most of us would be willing to deal with tremendous degradation and loss. I feel, unfortunately, that I went through an earlier lifetime of loss and degradation. I feel this is the time in my life to become me, and as much as I need to know that I will make it though the year, I need to not only see the light but to sit in its luminance and bask; and I'd rather not do it alone.

Mother and Child

Walking down the streets of New York could be easily compared to visiting the circus side shows of yore. There is simply currently nothing deemed unacceptable. There is nothing imaginable or unimaginable that cannot be seen in some billboard or shop window. There is nothing in way of vulgarities, open promiscuity, or of complete lowliness than cannot be uttered. The interesting thing is New Yorkers, being New Yorkers, don't appear rattled by their unseemly surroundings – they just keep going – not missing a beat.

It is with this outrageous background in mind, that I look at this social conundrum. Here we live in a society which by and large is unsurprised, unflustered, uninsulted, untouched by nearly anything and everything. We're surrounded by poverty, crime, and ugliness, to say nothing of a lack of personal physical respect and intimacy; and yet only the strangest things appear to get our ire.

My father, he should rest in peace, lived in a different era, a different time. Born in 1907, he remembered the influenza of the early twentieth century where they carried out the dead. He remembered water being brought in for baths in a big tub in the kitchen. He also remembered women, mothers, nursing babies on their front porches. The latter has always been one of his more interesting memories for me. After all, we're all pretty much aware of the relative recentness of in house plumbing and antibiotics; so his memories don't shock us; they merely serve as a reminder of how far we have come. But the breastfeeding on front porches – is that, too, a reminder, of where we came from – of how far we have come. If the addition of indoor plumbing allowed for warm baths in the privacy of our bathrooms and antibiotics and immunizations for the treatment and prevention of so much disease, what did the exit of the mothers breastfeeding on front porches provide?

As an animal lover, I have had the pleasure and privilege of observing animal mothers suckling their young. I am yet to see a human mother shielding her children's eyes from the site or a zoo keeper or pet owner removing this unspeakable physiological function from public view. And yet with the exit of these porch situated mothers, isn't that what society has done to women and human mammalia?

I nursed my own three children over two decades ago. During that time I was very involved with the educating, counseling, and encouraging of human lactation. It was a rebirth of a human's natural ability to feed her own young; it was also something that modern medicine, the pharmaceutical and baby food companies had largely taken over. History seems largely aware of that, if without a keen understanding of the reasons behind it. But with all that said, when, then, did nursing one's babies become such a dirty, disgusting function that it can only be hidden from public eye to be socially, and in some cases, even legally acceptable?

We live in an era where we rate the movies the public goes to see. Largely this has become a parental warning system, presuming that parents want it, heed it, or even are interested in the nature of what is being rated. The ratings are usually based on language, that is the type of words one is forced to hear as she/he walks the streets of New York, violence, the human relations one is treated to each night on the news – which you one can also find with very little effort in the streets of New York, and sexual content, which needless to say, overwhelm the individual walking through those very same streets.

So have nursing mothers of the late twenty and early twenty-first centuries been rated, too, is our concern for public decency? Well, let's see what we've been rated on? Language – seems unlikely – I've dealt with a lot of lactating women – can't say I remember any cursing whatsoever. Violence – hardly – studies have shown that nursing not only calms the mother and the baby – but the whole family around her also becomes sedated. Well, then it would appear that sexual content is all that remains. In a world where sex is revealed in store fronts and billboards, where men and women wear next to nothing at all, and where intimacy is the only thing that cannot be found on the screen – why has human lactation become the triple x threat?

Recently I overheard a young man recounting how his particular religious services have a rule that women are not allowed to nurse during services. I wondered now, whether men or women deemed inappropriately dressed were asked to leave, they were not, or if members using inappropriate language or bodily contact were also shown the doors. It seems that they weren't.

What is it then, about the human mammalian, and its use by the suckling young, that has become so abhorrent in the mere century from the scenes my father once knew?

In my study of Comparative Religious Thought I was delighted to find that the Greek Orthodox, in their effort to show the humanness of Mary, encouraged the painting of her nursing the Christ child. Were that not enough, there are legends of bits of dried milk saved as relics, just as pieces of the cross, martyred saints' bones, and vestiges of clothing were. The Roman Catholic Church was very uncomfortable with the humanness of Mary and much as they tried to stamp out the icons of the Greek Orthodox they, also, tried to leave little if any vestiges of humanity, and certainly of human sexuality, from the haloed Madonna. Nor is this an attack on the Catholic Church alone, for one finds the same disgust in the Evangelical Protestant Churches, in the Orthodox Jewish Synagogues, in many of the so called cults, and in much of the modern world as we know it.

If it were the word breast alone, that the modern world cannot accept, then the term Breast Cancer would hardly have been tarried about so successfully. Then what is it, pray tell. Surely, one sees very little of the actual breast during lactation, and most women take great care in covering the unoccupied member. Perhaps the disgust, the unacceptability, as is usually the case, can only be found in the eyes and mind of the beholder. Much as the Roman Catholic Church could not grant the envisioning of Mary as a human mother with breasts and sexuality; the beholders of abhorrent sexuality in the lactating women cannot bear the vision of women, mothers, as well as their own mothers, alone, as having breasts and inherent sexuality.

What this means, is that we can show sodomy, rape, and brutal beatings aplenty in cinemas worldwide, dress as if your body is for the world to behold; but do not feed your baby as biology designed you to, because there are those out there who cannot accept you as a woman, as a full human being.

Twenty-some odd years ago when I was fully involved in the lactation movement, I remember hearing the story of a woman who had to unexpectedly return to work after her child was born. Her boss, an unusually supportive individual, hung a picture of a mother and child above her desk.

There is something unspeakably tender about watching a mother animal suckling her young, there is something equally tender in each and every picture I have ever seen of Mary and the Christ child. This tenderness is found not one iota less in mothers nursing their infants today. Perhaps the idea has only to be rekindled in the minds of the viewers, of the world, as in the times of the ancients where Mary's humanness was put on a pedestal, and to where in more recent times a woman could proudly nurse her children on her own front porch.

Musings on Plates from Long Ago

Items owned over long periods of time have a habit of looking differently to us during different time periods. I think of my Pesach, that is Passover, dishware, for instance. During Pesach observant Jews clean their houses, the way homes were cleaned following plagues during the Middle Ages. And just when everything is shiny and perfect, the Pesach dishware is taken out.

In many cases, all these carefully hidden away items, were passed on from generation to generation; in my case, I bought almost all of them myself. As my family of origin wasn't observant and as my exhusband's family was neither generous nor overly taken with me; there was little other choice.

Over time, the collection grew. A simple salt and pepper and napkins holder set, some mugs given by a coworker from long ago, a canister set received when my exhusband drove us up to see some timeshares, upon the end of the sales line he cried poverty; true or not it was his preferable way of dealing with life. So we ended up with these

Pesach canisters and a salesman feeling sorry for us. The Milchig, dairy, dinnerware was slowly bought in one of those old time supermarket giveaways, where you bought a certain number of pieces per week. And gradually over time the collection grew until eventually, now on our own for years, I had to build three cabinets to contain them.

And so each year at Pesach we would proudly bring them out. My daughters getting a kick out of the young children's sets and cups; and I, just living in the feeling of playing house for a week. Oh, don't get me wrong, Pesach requires a lot of work, but there's something playful in taking out all these special memory laden items for just a week a year.

This year however, very much alone and disabled, I find the playfulness gone............Oh, each item still carries its memories but I'm not playing. Each year the bringing of Pesach has become much tougher and this year the tougher matched with the quiet and intense loneliness is making its own memorable images.

Pesach, to me, will always be those wonderful lengthy Sedorim, Seders, when everyone was home and we sang and talked way into the night. Sedorim, where due to the hour and my Multiple Sclerosis, there simply was no energy to finish washing the dishes until the morning after. Sedorim when young hands reached out to help me and where music filled the air.

The dishes still sit in front of me, basically, considering all the moving, intact, but there's no reaching hands and no music except my growingly hoarse voice. I still immediately note that both settings have a beige basis, that the very inexpensive stainless Milchig set still looks as good as new, that the adorable magnets cross stitched by a lovely art teacher, former coworker, of mine, still bring a bittersweet smile to my lips, that the ageless teakettle, looking somewhat embattled, still whistles. But this year, too, I wondered, if it was just time to turn it all over to the next generation, allowing them to make the next purchases, dream the next dreams, and form their own memories. When I moved here I didn't feel ready yet. I do now.

Oh, I'll miss having them here, knowing that they're all just waiting until the next Aviv, next springtime; but I would, also, know that they were being loved and cared for by those who had once reached out to help me and filled my life, memories, and Pesachim (Passovers) with song.

Dishes.

Of Things Owned and Missed

It's been over a year now, but it seems both longer and shorter. I moved from an apartment, that I had once loved, to one that would simply have to do. When I had moved to the prior apartment I had been downsizing, too, but it had been a pleasant, chosen – if you will – downsizing. I was giving up the apartment where my children had spent so many of their years, to a smaller one where I was hoping to spend a goodly number of mine. So my youngest daughter, my amanuensis, and I went through over a decade of holdings and made the garbage fields of Jersey richer. She would call me up at work repeatedly that summer, asking "can I throw this out?" It was more an order than a question, but I usually said yes. The fact is I didn't lose much I didn't want to and probably could have stood to lose more that she had suggested, to say nothing of those things she feared too highly to ask.

This move was very different. For one thing, most everything would have to be placed in storage for half a month until the apartment would be ready; for another, this time I needed a lot of help.

In preparation for the prior move, we drove around and around until finding exactly what I was looking for. I felt in control – in command. Everything fell right into place. We even had several days to carry over everything we didn't want handled by the movers. It was an organized, good feeling move. It even took less time and cost less money than the movers had estimated – a virtual unknown entity!

This time was different. My closet case of Multiple Sclerosis was out in the open. I couldn't drive and I was using a cane to walk. My youngest daughter, once again, helped by calling in friends to move me into storage. My middle daughter and her family permitted me to stay with them until the new place was ready.

Even though we had paid well in advance, the new management company wouldn't release the keys until the commencement of the lease – a situation I have never encountered previously. The movers and I literally sat in front of the building waiting for maintenance to arrive, keys in hand. Once here, they insisted that I sign that everything was alright - Everything wasn't alright – There was only one set of keys and the kitchen cabinets hadn't been cleaned adequately.

The night after I moved into the previous apartment, I slept like a baby – It just fit so well. The night after I moved in here – I barely slept at all. I ALL of a sudden I was afraid A RAT or a burglar or rapist would appear from nowhere – None did – They have yet to appear. The new train the next day – My new method of transportation - was dirty and filled with difficulties for one with physical disabilities.

And for a nonmaterialist, I found myself missing the mountain of items that we had to get rid of due to space consideration – I felt I had thrown out my memories. I kept picturing my daughters' dollhouse – the one they had put together - and all the Purim costumes. There was also the matter of losing my daughter's bedroom – She of course would always be welcomed in my home – but she no longer had a room of her own here.

I've known people who have lost and regained fortunes – they had their stories - but my pain of losing memories seems hurtful to the quick - in a way that money - an item with no inherent value - isn't......................

My old home proved to have it holes – there was the ceiling heating that caused the ceiling to peel, there was the neighbor, who moved in six months before I left, who was lewd and loud; and there was the community, which when the schools became more crowded and new sewers required construction, as well, decided to lash out at the tenant community members. Yet all and all, it had been largely six years of bliss – a nice place that I had chosen and felt empowered – a beautiful site to open up into each morn as my cats and I peered out into the porch; each morning when I open the blinds here, I miss my porch. Here – I have been trying to make a home – I try to make the dwelling – what the building is not – clean, safe, livable, and homey. I have my fears – but I carry them with me.

I may always miss those items I couldn't keep – but other moves took memories away from me as well. A writer collects her memories and writes them to the world, I guess singers sing them, and artists paint theirs. There is no perfect existence, as we live we lose, we also gain. To live means to hurt – If we're lucky it also means to love – I've done both. In the East, they talk a lot about Nirvana – about the release of all suffering – they talk of living with complete equanimity – but what they're really speaking of is detachment – and I've never been detached – the pain of loss means to have once owned – I've lost friends – I'm glad I had them. One tries to learn from one's losses - gleaning what can be gained from the sad and the bad and the memories. One doesn't always get to chose one's losses – they frequently choose us and yet – Loss means having lived as much as gain does.

In the end, I'm still sitting here tonight writing – I'm warm and fed and my cat's nearby. And my youngest daughter still turns the world over to help me.

Primitiveness

You knew it was going to happen; or at least I did. They call it 'Political Correctness', I call it stupidity. It started with him/her/or it. Then all nouns had to be desexed or sexually pluralized. History had to be rewritten. One Pre-School director, I worked under, instructed teachers, one Thanksgiving, not to dress the Native American costumed students in beads and feather. 'Why not I queried', egging her on, 'Because they didn't dress that way', she sighed. 'Of course they did', I smirked. I went on 'And the Pilgrims, how are we to dress the Pilgrims'. 'Oh, you can dress them as usual, I was told.'

But the bologna continues. I had a highly intelligent, but volatile, female student in my Ethics class. Every time we read from the textbook, she would stop and reassign the pronouns. Finally one day, when discussing prisons, she did it again. You like women to be imprisoned, I queried. She stared. I went on, I told her what I knew about women prisoners; and then asked her if this was what she really wanted for women.

Of course, the Bard William Shakespeare, as well as all writers of fine literature, continue to turn in their graves. Must we disturb their sleep over this stupidity!

But as I feared, it didn't end there. I knew eventually art would be attacked. Well, the other day in the newspaper, I saw it – the relabeling of ancient arts – the removal of the term 'Primitive' – I'd scream – but I knew it was coming; so I laughed, halfheartedly.

The article was not at all persuasive. In fact, it was downright pathetic. It described Ancient African and Oceanic Art – the journalist could come up with no better adjective – so merely sighed and called them 'beautiful'. Well, for Pete's Sake! No one ever said that they weren't, but they were still primitive. Works done by preliterate, prehistoric people, by hand or with simple tools. There is nothing ugly about them, but they remain primitive.

There is much to be done in the real world to improve life for all beings. This includes all races, religions, both genders, as well as everything that walks, flies above, or swims the waters of this earth; but relabeling changes nothing. Changing beautiful simply written literature doesn't change it. Rewriting history to read what we would have preferred to have happen, doesn't change it; and labeling objects as being other than they are, certainly doesn't change it.

It is never easy to change society, but lies and misnomers won't do it. Want to help someone? Help someone help him or himself. This isn't done by changing the truth; this is done by hard work and above all else, the desire to change. I see nothing of that in this 'Politically Correct' garbage – nothing at all.

The Poor Minority – A Wonderment

Living amongst the impoverished minority, I feel both imprisoned and enschooled. I'm largely uncomfortable with their loudness, the incessant smoking that fills the halls, albeit illegally now. The foul language, the inappropriate dress, the slovenliness of it all. The habit of leaving something, anything, where it fall or lay. The seemingly lack of desire to move on or up. And indeed living here, amongst them, leaves me with a sense of impoverishness, lowness, inappropriateness, slovenliness; even when I run off to work before the sun rises and work lengthy hours. Even when I work against the limits of my disabled body to keep my unit, apartment, home – if you will, clean. And yet I'm permitted the luxury of a live in learning experience, one that few research programs would have provided access equally.

I can't help making the continual comparison, of the early twenty – late nineteen century European and Asian immigrants, who within one generation, sent their children into the professions, businesses, and middle classhood. Sure it can be argued; it's harder now. And yet my brother-in-law, born circa nineteen-sixties, was born first generation Chinese American. His family came to California and worked like dogs, his father died young. And, yet, he went to Yale, his brother became a photographer. We see Supreme Court Justice Sotomayor do the same thing; coming from New York housing projects. It can be done, even now. The question is why it isn't. Why would anyone choose this lowness?!

I remember a counselor, in theory, trying to advise me, a young divorced mother of three, to leave Jewish Orthodoxy largely to obtain wealth. She made it clear my choice, not to leave, disgusted and infuriated her; that I had chosen poverty.

The differences, if you will, are great between the two choices illustrated. The former that of minorities, choosing to move not ahead, to learn not from other members of the society; and leaving their families through, hunger, drug abuse, alcoholism, adolescent sex and promiscuity, crime, and early death. The latter, a chance to live in a small firm community where children are brought up to believe, against the world at large, that THERE IS something more out there than meets the eye. In lieu of crime, misery, and lowness, the children are brought up with morality, education, and continual striving towards something higher. True my children did not have a lot, but they never went clothesless or hungry. They didn't go without medical care, books, or learning. The difference is great.

Perhaps the counselor never looked at what I, as an individual, chose to give up to give my children this – how working in a small minded and sometimes mean place, allowed me to watch my children grow and interact with them. So, while I was underemployed, I was never unemployed; and while I was employed, my children were never latch key children.

Those surrounding me, in the building I sometimes call home, have made no such decision. Indeed, it appears that the decision, they may well have made, was not to act – not to decide, a forgone conclusion if you will – of hopelessness.

Community based societies, seem to offer their people a kind of home, a level of support, that seems to be missing here. Oh, the 'Hood', as this group is known to call their neighborhoods, appears to support things too – but largely harmful ones – bootlegging cigarettes, videotapes, cds, and anything else that can be knocked off cheaply. Alcohol and drug abuse is legion. Sexuality affront you, as in probably no other place. Little girls can expect to be sexually abused by their relatives, their parents' 'friends', and ESPECIALLY their mothers' endless line of boyfriends.

This is surely a different kind of poverty than my children experienced. This is surely a different poverty than the European and Asian immigrants, immersed in tenements, experienced. The question we are forced to ask, is why.

The Black Community has been excusing this endless poverty system as the dividend of American Slavery; but I for one, don't buy it. Have you known an Afro-American slave, no; why, because Slavery died with the Civil War. Were there problems, certainly, but not slavery. And yet, over one hundred years later the Afro-American Community continues to blame slavery.

There is a Biblically based teaching known in the Jewish Orthodox Community. They teach that when the Jews left Egypt although 'freed', that they were still of a slave mentality; that the real reason that they waited forty years before entering Israel, was so they could die out and the next generation enter as 'freemen'. Now what is the difference here, we still see the mention of slave mentality; but it's not seen as endless, as eroding future generations, or progress. Indeed, it was viewed as ending with that generation.

Where then is the difference? One could argue that much of the Afro-America Community still fought, and in some ways, still fights the burden of the skin colored bias. And yet, we have an Afro-American president, there are Afro-American millionaires, business successes and scholars, professionals, and it goes on. In addition, Jews worldwide, did not have a piece of cake handed them when they left Egypt, either. Jews were hated and prosecuted as far back as we know and continue to be today.

Obviously the difference is both self image and community. It's also important to note, that although Blacks and Jews notoriously marched together in this country's Civil Rights Movements, that afterwards the Afro-Americans walked away angry at the Jews; no doubt angry that the Jews went ahead to do better in society at large. There is no question that Jews did; however, that doesn't mean they did so at the Black man's loss or burden. Jews did better partially because their religion, unlike the Black man's skin, is not as obvious a source of prejudice. Much like light skinned blacks, they passed through.

But surely the perspective doesn't end there, because, there were Afro-Americans who emerged differently from the Civil Rights Movement – they watched the Jews and learned from them, they learned

Renée M. Ducker - 140

the importance of education, family, and hard work; indeed they invented Kwanzaa, based on Chanukah and Jewish familial celebrations. These Afro-Americans made huge strides and became part of mainstream America.

Too many of the others, have not. Instead they stay on the street at night, loud, angry, inappropriate, and with unrealistic and meaningless dreams; they hurt themselves, they hurt each other, they stagnate and die. I'm convinced it doesn't have to be this way, but a person has to want to change. Just as you can only lead the horse to the source of water, you can only help another being just so much; at some point, he or she MUST want to help himself.

Reminiscences of Pesachs* Past

Unexpectedly disabled from a heretofore benign condition, I sit

here staring at the Fleishig (meat) salt and pepper shakers; filled but left

unused. My Pesachs became disconnected, lone individual pursuits, after

my eldest and middle children had married and the youngest had gone

off to college. Now with my physical limitations growing, I can no

longer run from store to store in search of just the RIGHT Pesach item;

in its stead, I must have a supermarket delivery service search my items

out – the best they can. The days of scrubbing everything from floors to

walls are gone as well; with Rabbinical Blessing, I was told to only 'do

what I can'. Each Pesach would feel that much less like Pesach to me. I

spent Seder (Passover ritual meal) after Seder alone. Reading the

Haggadah (Seder book), singing the songs; I did the Mitzvos

(duties/laws/good deeds), but enjoyed no company. I was very much

alone. This year in a new abode, where I am just beginning to develop a

community; I feel even THAT much more isolated. Then suddenly an

old friend and his wife invited me for a Seder. In my old abode this was done continually, I just turned them down; but here I feel differently – I surprised myself by saying "YES".

Their Seder was lovely. They made me feel much at home. It wasn't our family Seder. It wasn't my family. But it was a Seder. They're my friends and I felt at home. In my effort to gain a foot in trying to make my current life situation work for me, I've learned that I must walk a different path than the one that took me through all these years. I can no longer proudly say "I can do it ALONE", because I no longer can. The emptiness of the Pesach week are not unlike many other facets of my current era. My nest is empty and NOW I can't even fly. The dishes sit here largely unused. The memories beckon; but they sadden me. It occurred to me to give my Pesach stores away when I moved; but I wasn't ready then and I find that I'm not ready now. One day they'll fashion someone else's table, BUT NOT YET.

Chol Ha Moed (the middle holiday days) allowed me the time to run around shopping and museum experiencing. I really enjoyed it, but it took incredible effort and I went WAY OVER budget; I can't help but wondering whether I was running away from my isolating cell.

My Pesach Vacation is almost up and yet I feel no desire to return to work; the place I go merely to cover my rent and living costs.

No more than the isolation, this meaningless work doesn't define me, either.

My life, at this juncture, confounds me with its challenges, as well as the questions it poses. Having been a single parent all those years, I never planned to be a middleaged single woman spending my life alone. When the children were home, I didn't have the time or space to be lonely. Now I have no other. Each stage in life challenges the individual to change and grow. I can only ask the G-d above to grant me the ability at this point, when I feel physically spent and emotionally overwhelmed; when my children are far away - making their lives what they should be.

The infamous Haggadah song that the children love and the grown ups loathe, called Dayenu, speaks of all the gifts that G-d has given us. In singing it, we repeatedly affirm that the item mentioned in the prior verse would have been sufficient in itself. Here I am making it on my own. Here I am safe, clothed, sheltered, and fed. Here I am with a Holiday vacation; and yet it doesn't feel sufficient.

I do not know what tomorrow will bring. I can only hope to make it better. But for now, the Pesach dishes surround me – crying out "Look at me, use me, where is everyone?". Indeed where is everyone?

Looking across the empty rooms filled with my memories, cat, and self, I must evidently find the fullness – the sufficiency – to inspire myself as I endeavour to build a community – endeavour to build a life not spent alone.

Chag Sameach. (Happy Holiday.)

* Pesach is the Hebrew/Yiddish word for Passover.

Autumnal Rituals

To many, rituals bring to mind anachronistic images of long ago religions and civilizations. Something resembling an eighth grade social studies textbook, perhaps. something that speaks of dogma, old wives tales, and yesteryear. Yet in reality, rituals are far more than that; they're the very fabric that makes up life and the memories we hold so dear. I find this again and again as I engage in my study in Comparative Religious Thought; and I find this again and again as I look back into my own memories as a mother, now grandmother, as I engage in life. What follows are one mother's picture of rituals, her memories of rituals, and how rituals shape our very lives.

When two people marry there are many unexpressed expectations on both sides; these unexamined and unshared expectations are based on childhood rituals. If two people marry from different cultures or religions their ritual expectations will be that much wider; frequently this shows up more when the children come and baptisms, brisim (religious Jewish circumcision and naming) are sweetly remembered and the desire for repetition and meaning come to the forefront of the bearer's mind, actions, and wishes. Up to that time sharing traditions, rituals, was fine; now, with the children, the next generation, fully present, the feelings are different. Responsibility for repetition of childhood rituals come to the forefront; and there's no holding back.

In many ways as a single parent, my life was easier. There were no arguments over parenting, life styles, schooling, religion, or ritual. In addition, my upbringing, in an antireligion, antinational background household, held little in the way of ritual, so I, as a parent, had to invent them as I went.

The calendar, when permitted, presents the participant which such an opportunity. Much as many holidays have at least some calendarial aspect, so each month, season, and nature/weather event presents the living with a chance for a response in kind.

If you start with autumn, which I tend to, as it is the season of Rosh Hashanah and Yom Kippur, the Jewish New Year; the newly crisp autumn air and leaf colours seem to cry out for a response. The first ritual that comes to mind to me though is the opening of school. This, in many ways is strange for an individual who as a child hated nothing more. Indeed I went to school kicking and screaming and slept through it until the humanities beckoned to me in high school. Yet school's

opening is where I begin my memories of my growing family's rituals.

School always brought in a flurry of activities. There were new clothes

and shoes to buy. There was the never ending list of somehow inviting,

to say nothing of expensive, school supplies to acquire. There were the

musings of which teacher and which course of study, as well; but that

was almost secondary in nature. No, it was the physical renewal of

ourselves; the haircuts, the clothing, the new acquisitions that made the

time special. Many a day was spent finding the items, writing the lists,

and then of course, once home, arranging everything just right. This

skirt with this pair of socks, this folder with this looseleaf, special new

pencils in this container. It was with this sense of joy and wonder, that

my children entered school each year. Sure they might not have been

given their favourite teacher, or perhaps a friend was in another class or

had even moved away. Perhaps life was not perfect at home. There may

not have been enough of this or that and financial basic security was

never as assured as with friends of two parent families; and yet when it

came to school preparations, they were all there. Their far more affluent

friends might not have gotten all their folders on time but my children

were sure to have had them. Their more affluent friends were apt to be

pulled out of school to choose that coat or skirt; but not my children, they were there with everything they needed ready for whatever the school

year would hold. Perhaps their home could be pulled out from under

them, perhaps they couldn't always buy everything they wanted or

needed from the supermarket; but when it came to school SOMEHOW

everything was there. It was an autumnal school year ritual that spelled

security and led to an academic comfort zone. Two of my children

would even prove to become unusually capable scholars; and even the

third, within her limitations, would still go far.

Rituals

On several appointed nights of the week, regardless of the length of my day, the oil in my hair, the bills in the mail, the messages on the machine, or the state of society itself, I sit down in the corner of my livingroom and sign onto MSN. Locating myself onto Yahoo's mail site, I type in my password and pass over to the other side.............I'm with my baby again......................

Other children might prefer the phone, mine prefers email. I carefully read and reread her messages - as with each word, each letter, I can hear the sweet sound of her voice. I then compose my letter to her, detailing the funny and not-so-funny moments of my day. Taking care not to forget the goings on of the cat and his world. Some days our musings are long, other short and to the point, some serious, others merely amusing. But all written with love and longing.

Normally I am not a computer person, preferring, instead, the simple and nondigital objects of our world. But with my daughter, the screen is transcribed into another essence - a world where two adult females can be together for moments at a time, though hundreds of miles apart.

Through the screen too, I see our lives developing fully and separately as they should - but with the continual touching of our hearts..........

As a young girl, I loved letters, as well. Purchasing beautiful and interesting stationery items. I was always writing to others far and near. Even today, receiving a letter is special. But I can remember no letter that filled me with the same joy or tearfulness as this odd modern means of communication, as this one that my daughter has chosen.

Just as once knowing that she was safe in bed, or knowing that she was well and unharmed, filled me with the traditional parental warmth; the hearing of her computerized voice now does the same. And rather than cheapening the feeling, it deepens it.

Surely with time, her time allotments will lessen, and I may well have to confine myself to fewer message units. But surely as with each musical movement, they will be chock filled with meaning and emotion; and they will always be welcome.

Sanity

Sometimes our very sanity stands on the mere hold of a hand, sound of a voice, or word on a page. It may not seem a lot to stand on, but at highly emotionally charged moments; it may be all there is. On the other hand, what drove us off kilter, may not have been very much more – a word, a letter, a sound; sometimes that is all that it can take to unhinge oneself from the sanity doorframe.

I remember one time remarking to my youngest daughter, at a key point in her young life, that sometimes just one word can change everything. In the positive that can be a yes – that can be an invitation, that can be an opening. It can easily be the key that that opens up worlds to you. Such is the insanity – when one word, one letter, one sound, one touch – seems to close them all down.

Sanity –

The bare thread

That stands between you and me

The word that holds me together

The nod

The voice

On the one hand

It's everything that's good with the world

On the other

Without it

There's no sunshine

I can make it without bread

Without money

Without all the things

That are said to run the world

But without you

There's nothing

There's darkness

With no hope of light

It's a bare thread

Merely a word, a hand, or a look

But it's all I have

It's all there is.

Sanity.

Social Evolution

Most people accept some of Darwin's Evolutionary Theory; whether through basic understanding or long term held public viewpoint. Furthermore, most people accept some form of basic psychology; once again through a very fundamental comprehension and general public standing. In the understanding of sociological, anthropological, and historical growth there is a general viewpoint, as well, that there was gradual growth through the centuries, up and down as it may have been, leading us, humankind, to where we are now (G-d help us!!!). It is with this general understanding, that I offer you the following...................

I have never been politically correct; I'm not starting now. In the decades since political correctness dawned/was forced upon us some academic terms became passé – or up for censure. The term primitive comes to mind. I remember working in a preschool in which the director came to speak to us, one year, instructing us to ditch the traditional Native American garb in our model Thanksgiving dinner. I remember asking her if we were to ditch the garb of the Pilgrim fathers as well – and was told – no, OF COURSE NOT. Anthropologists, historians, and sociologists now, when referring to nonwriting societies, have nixed the term primitive as well – They're different – they're artistic – They communicated thought in alternative styles. One of the general terms for certain kinds of art is primitive as well – I can't wait to see what's been done with that...............................

The only problem with this correctness is that it belies the truth. We don't look at children during the preliterate age as complete – they're uneducated/il/preliterate – We don't want them to stay that way – We expect growth into literacy. Yet we look at preliterate societies and see them as equal to literate ones. I'm not referring to some Stone Age era peoples. I'm talking about peoples who came through the eras where other peoples communicated through letters and numbers and they did not. I'm talking about people, who while others built aqueducts, sewer systems, and buildings, they continued drinking unpurified water and living in thatched huts. I'm talking about people who, excepting for commercial items thrown to them by the civilized world, live pretty much as they did thousands and thousands of years ago. We can sit here and say that these people are communicating and producing in other ways, but how? We can say they are beautiful peaceful pastoral people. Yet this isn't always true. Sometimes they're warlike savages – a word nixed close to a century ago. Frequently they're malnourished with high maternal/infantile fatalities. Usually as soon as they have any interaction with the civilized world, they contract illness and die as they have no immunizations or effective medical care.

These insights can be found in far less foreign soil, as close to home as the local inner cities. In the news, we are barraged with statistics of how inner city children are doing in school. Well, look at their parents. Their parents are part and parcel of their own primitive societies, if you will. Immigrants who come to this country and make no effort to learn the language are cursing their children with ignorance and illiteracy, poverty, crime, and hopelessness; and all this needlessly. Immigrants came to this country, as to all other countries, through the history of this earth. They learned the languages and customs of their newly acquired homes and went onto grow. Some even did better than the surrounding natives. It is not politically correct to call these culturally inept people primitive; but what would you prefer - stupid/ignorant/idiots???

You don't even have to look to foreign tongues for social backwardness. There are people in the inner city faring little better. No, they speak English – Their own slant on it – call it 'Street'.......... Their children, too, fail. Coming from homes where there is no child care, no consistent quality food, where daddy is frequently absent and mommy sleeps with one boyfriend after another in the next room. And this is to say nothing of when the children leave the uninhabitable dwelling each morning; how can you do well in school, when you're terrified to walk down the hallway or street because they're full of violent drug users and sex offenders?

A colleague of mine, whose children attend a local school system, complained how low the level of education was. Public school traditionally aimed at the average – the average has lowered, and in response to ignorant political pressure, the aim is for the lowest. She told me that her children read – but that they didn't learn it at school. Of course not, I counseled. Children of readers read; children of the illiterate don't.

Recently a study was done and publicized on the whole reading program – as opposed to phonetic ones. The findings were incorrectly publicized as showing the program as incapable of teaching children to read. What it really showed was that children from reading homes learned to read; children from nonreading, did not. This wasn't a politically correct finding; so it was eschewed.

In medicine we can't afford political correctness. Certain national, racial, and social backgrounds produce higher percentages of certain diseases or conditions. Lying about it won't change the facts.

Doctors slowly learned in the early modern era, that if they washed their hands patients did better. Successful immigrants found that if they learned the language and ways of their new countries, that they would slowly succeed. Good students learn that if they follow instructions and listen to their teachers, and do the work, that they will surely succeed. Why haven't these social groups learned. What are they learning? Why are we dealing with it by lying?

In looking at early human history, let's look at the variety of early hominids which didn't survive, most likely it was their inability to evolve effectively that took its toll. We're dealing with such societies now; the problem is we're permitting them to destroy society as a whole. Through political correctness, we're not only lying to them; but lying to ourselves as well.

Summer's End

I am saddened by summer's end,

All seems possible in summer

All one's dreams and hopes can come to fruition,

can come true, can come to pass;

Perhaps like a child's dream,

Or, no, more like a thought, wish, or belief

from earlier times;

The sun rises, the skies blue,

Everything is green and bright,

The earth is warm,

And we are free to roam amongst her;

I miss summer,

And she is yet to leave.

Time, Speed, and Beating Einstein's Time

Observing children, just yesterday, which is what I did for a living for so many years, I realized that the difference between our childhood memories and those of our children is not all this technology. Oh, no what follows is hardly a diatribe against technology. So, you Techies out there can calm down! What marks this tremendous demarcation is our vastly different sensing of time. Indeed, some of my fondest and most meaningful memories growing up consisted of the very timelessness of my childhood. Days, weeks, and months where I could just contemplate life, a tree branch, a book, a dream, another person. I did not wear a watch until adolescence and except for school (which I dreaded) and doctor and dental visits (ditto) time mattered not. Summer was a time to dream, to walk untethered to schedules. Each school day's end marked a tremendous whiff of freedom - the freedom to be - to think - to stare. Each holiday, each evening, each night, a time to look into the future, to pretend, to wonder.

I watch this generation, as I've said, and I've watched them for well over two decades now. They run about tethered to a schedule involving a time and space competition that our generation never knew.

Small children - under three - the ones we once referred to as toddlers -

now toddle not; instead they are dragged to Mommy and Me class, Early

Swimmers' Class, Tiny Aerobics Class, etc., etc.. Kindergarteners must

have afterschool enrichment programs (and some even have homework).

First graders now tote home backpacks so heavy that there are regular

articles in every family oriented periodical suggesting backpack

stratagem. And by the time a child hits middle school (which in some

school systems is dangerously close to fourth or fifth grade) children are

already chafing under the fears of not making it into the Ivy Leagues.

A parent recently proudly described her son's summer schedule -

four weeks of basketball camp, three weeks of soccer camp, and three

weeks of water sport camp. She then chuckled about the expense (hardly

a problem in her late baby boomer affluence). But the one expense, she

had never counted on, was the cost to her child. Four plus three plus

three add up to an entire summer of scheduling. There was no family

time, no exploring time, no down time, and no HIM TIME. The boy

received a summer void of anytime for or of himself

My own childhood was not basked in baby boomer affluence;

my two professional parents were many things, but never affluent. Nor were they prefect parents in any idealized picture; but what they (and my era on a whole) did allow for, was free time. I had time to create in time and space and time to choose not to. I had time to get to know my neighbors and peers, time to learn to roam my neighborhood (something today's affluent suburban children rarely do). But most of all, I had time to get to know me. Now I have to say (Caveat Emptor) that my parents were not exactly thrilled with the 'me' I got to know and explore; but nonetheless, I did know who I was and what that meant to me. In years to come, other psychologists and philosophers may argue over how I (for instance) spending several weeks trying to reawaken a dead or dying branch in my own backyard, was or was not a good use of time. But for me, the point is time didn't matter.

I remember when we were preparing for the engagement of my middle child (my eldest daughter) I noted that my biggest announcement to my household was to have my future son-in-law's family's phone number installed into the memory of our telephone system. What? That's an announcement? Well, yes, in a generation which is seemingly working against time, that is a very apropos one. It simply says that reaching my daughter's fiance-to-be has become so important that we must beat time in order to do so.

I think, also, outside of my family. A highly intelligent colleague of mine, has recently joined an office where I am employed. Basically she turned down one position in order to be accepted for the other. However, what she really wants to do is to do both - multitasking; thereby earning two salaries simultaneously. Is it possible? Well, yes, in that particular line of work - computing - she can indeed do both; and being the capable professional that she is - she no doubt will! But who will bear the cost? Oh, no, I'm not concerned about her employers having to pay the same person simultaneously for the same timeslot. (My sympathies lie decidedly elsewhere.) My concern is for her children and herself. Multitasking is a phrase used to describe both modern work techniques as well as the pattern where women (especially mothers) attempt and succeed in performing several different tasks simultaneously. Yes, I too, remember, nursing my youngest, frying eggs, and talking on the phone - directing some sort of volunteer cause - simultaneously. At that time, while harried, I felt proud - look at me SUPERMOM - I could do it all! Now I look back and realize, that the call could have waited - or gone to others - the other two children could have had cereal - and I could have nursed the last of my trio quietly, graciously, cooing away!

Recently, I've been hearing about all these experiments

involving beating the speed of light. Let me let you know that my areas of expertise do not include science. But I am interested - so I listen. First, we are told that it is largely theoretical – that no one has yet succeeded in REALLY moving something - anything - beyond the speed of light; however experimentation is taking place. I have to say I have always been interested in scientific research; and as a former psychological researcher, I am not surprised that this is the generation to take on time. After all, with all our children's schedules, and all our multitasking, all our phone calls, and all our highly competitive aims - if we don't beat the speed of light, we may not get there. And yet the interesting thing about all this research - was the theory that by breaking this time barrier that we are actually moving back in time. Wow! Could that be? With all this hurrying, with all this competition, with all these goals, could we really be going in reverse? And, moreover, if this is indeed the case, would slowing down put us back on target again? I really don't know, but I am considering becoming watchless once more.

To My Daughter

This essay is dedicated to my daughter, who is always afraid that if I give her too much, I will somehow end up with nothing…

Dear Tzippi,

Unlike the glass from which you drink, the human heart cannot be emptied; oh, don't get me wrong it can spill, crack, and bleed, but for as long as it beats, it will always be full.

Oh, I know that your concern is that the little money we have will permanently and adversely be affected by any joyful expenditure on your behalf. You worry that I/We will not 'make it' – whatever 'it' is – if we buy you a pretty new sweater or a needed bookbag or book. But what is money for anyway….only bills? NO!

Oh, I know that I have bills to pay, rent to make, obligations to make good. But you seem to forget that my first obligation is to you.

I have gone without a great many things in the course of my life. I have faced hunger, loss of home, and loss of those I've loved. So, I am not blind or dumb or naively brave. I have also braved tough waves before and somehow I have always kept the breath within my lungs; and although, I do not take credit for this alone, it does leave me with an enormous faith.

For your information, I do not get scared, when I buy you a pair of sneakers or jacket or theatre tickets. I get scared when I can't. I get scared when I can find no earthly way to meet your meagre needs. One of my saddest times in my life, was not being able to buy you a gift for Chanukah. In contrast, one of my bravest days, was signing the contract to send you to M.K.A. – oh, I gave them my last $1,000.00 and had no idea where the rest was coming from....But I didn't care....I didn't care 'cause I knew it was the right thing to do. Even now, I look at it as my shining hour. When I took you to see RENT, I got you orchestra seats, which I could scarcely afford, but it didn't matter, 'cause you needed to be there.

No, my worries are never spent on what I do for you, but rather on what I cannot. My greatest days, are those that I can give to you...those which show me that I can make a difference in your life......A life (by the way) which I know will make a difference in the world......JUST BY BEING YOU......

Yesterday, when I took you shopping, my feelings were only of your pleasures, my worries – for those I could not supply.

Somehow I will make the rent and pay the utilities, the creditors, the loans, and what-have-you, but life is short – allow me the pleasure of giving you joy.

Your Loving Maaaaaaaaaa,

Im

Too Darn Fast

I think back three decades and I remember a friend who, upon accepting a position in an engineering library, described her first task of each day. She would come in and pick up a pile of requests. She would then prioritize them. The ones labeled A.S.A.P. would go the top; as she understood then to be time sensitive. Every once in a whole, however, one would be labeled P.D.Q., 'pretty darn quick'; those she would decidedly put at the very bottom of the pile with those that she might or might not reach by day's end.

We live in a growingly impolite society. The computer, the expedited delivery services, the twenty-four hour stores and businesses, and the lack of blue laws, the monsters that we created, largely put us there. No matter where you wait on line these days, someone comes in placing him or herself in front of all those who had arrived before and announcing that she/he cannot wait. Well, why not? Children accompanying adults on such lines create holy terror, because no one has taught them that lines are part of human existence. Cashiers, clerks, office secretaries, telephone operators and any other middle person sit on the receiving end of this madness. People have come to feel ABOVE waiting. Others can wait for them; but not they for others, or anything for that matter.

Nor is this to say that computers, expedited delivery, or anything open beyond the old norm is bad in themselves. They are not; but like much else in life, it's not so much something in itself, but rather what is done with it. What we've done with it, is to become a society of entitlement. I touch a button on the computer and the screen reads 'done'. Super, but if you're asking a person to carry something out, it is bound to take somewhat longer. A person is not a computer. In addition, a faulty computer now leads adults to respond with two year old type temper tantrums as they CANNOT WAIT!

The other day, in my day job, a client asked something of me. Then before even completely telling me what he desired, he wanted to know the time length of the task. I can only breathe a sigh of relief that Bach, Beethoven, Leonardo da Vinci, and Tolstoy never had such ogres as bosses; they surely would never had been able to leave us the legacy with timetables such as there are now.

There is much to say for knowing immediately what's in your checking account, for the immediate email response of a colleague, for the name of that book from your researcher; but there was much to say for waiting as well. In the midst of our computerness, I still love the feel and sight of beautiful stationery and stamps. I still send them out in the snail mail world and eagerly await a reply in kind. In most cases, I could easily email the individual, but I prefer not to. If it's an urgent situation, the phone and email still exist; but in most cases it is not. Letter writing gives both the reader and the writer the time to savour words and to think long and hard about how the other person and the communications being shared do matter. Emails are barely grammatical and more often than not thoughtless. I doubt many would have the guts to say on paper or person what they manage to put online. This is of course not Cyrano shyly writing a letter to his beloved Roxanne. This is about the frequently, clumsy, rude and unfeeling words that pass unedited from one's screen to the other.

People have ceased to regard time as anything but an order to create. I heard one idiot business owner yellowing at a manager that he didn't want his workers to be doing nothing – he was unabashedly angry that the computer system was down and that they had to wait until the I.T. department brought it up again. The I.T. director, on hand, tried to explain to him that these momentary snags in the system took a mere three minutes to overcome; for this two year old tyrant, three minutes was more than he could bear.

There are educators and parents, these days, who can't pile enough schoolwork and afterschool activities on top of children. They see a moment's free time as the devil's workshop. They should have met an old friend of mine, a Rabbi who lived out in the country on a large free range pastoral lot. In the summer, he, even though saddled as a single parent for many years, refused to send his brood to camp. He understood their need to space out. We're depriving our children of this time to dream and think things out. Who knows what they'd be inventing, or writing, or painting in their heads; but no, instead we have them working on twenty more math problems or engaging in twenty more basketball dribbling practices.

I remember taking a walk one holiday morning and seeing a small group of people assembled outside the Post Office. They could not come to grips with the idea that the institution was closed for the holiday. Telephone answering service operators find the same enigma when clientele call for doctors and lawyers off hours and are met with disbelief and anger upon informing them that the offices are closed. There are simply no nonbusiness hours any longer. Children in an earlier era were said to have thought that their teachers lived in school at night. It's almost as if today's adult clientele think that their physicians and attorneys live in their offices, too.

When I was growing up, I was taught that you didn't call someone after 9:30 at night or before 9:00 in the mornings during the week or 11:00 on the weekends. Today no time is safe; people feel they can interrupt your life for their 'important' calls at anytime at all. If their calls were of real importance that might be alright; but they frequently are of no importance except to the caller him/herself.

When we teach a child to wait on line or that something he/she wanted has not come in the mail today; we are teaching her/him something more important than how to handle that moment. We are teaching her how to handle life, itself. A wise physician once told me that doctors didn't know how to wait; that midwives were much better at it. Perhaps we're in need of more midwifery today. We're in need of a rebirth of free and waiting times. We need businesses to close. People need time when they can't be reached and the only others they can reach out to are friends and family. It was argued, decades ago, that blue laws were from a different era of religious stronghold in this world and country. The fact is regardless of your religious, or lack there of, affiliation, blue laws allowed a day off for many who would have had none without it. In today's society, where we have to work longer and harder to hold ourselves together; a day where everything closed would be a blessing regardless of whether you do or do not choose to worship.

Each of us is only one person, but in our little ways we can help bring the sanity back. Thank the clerk when you are waited on. Allow your client to express her /himself completely and give him plenty of time letting her know that you're there for him. Sleep in sometime and give up an errand or two; the world won't end. Next time you're driving, take another turn and drive down a pretty road. Get out and look around. The world hasn't ended. It just got better!

The Waiting Game

Women have always been thought of as the more patient of the species. For centuries, that may have been explained away by their supposed inherent docility as opposed to the assumed greater aggression of their male counterparts. Over the last hundred years or so, women have been reassessed as to their gender inherent traits. Indeed, gender inherent traits are still being readdressed in this regard; and perhaps with some very good reasons. However, patience may have some very real, rather than romanticized reasons, for its historical connection with the female gender; and these reasons, twenty-first century and all, maybe no less true than in former times.

Women due to their biology, due to their gender, have been programmed to wait. This waiting starts early, as the young girl yearns to mature physically; right away this is something she can not control – she must wait. Then, once menarche has started, she will then spend the next thirty to forty years waiting each month for the sign /reminder of her femininity, her fecundity, her empty womb. There are all sorts of anti-conceptual devices on the market today, and yet she still waits for

Nature's say; and in an era where she need not do this, studies seem to point to the fact, that most women would prefer this wait.

As this young girl becomes a woman and the childbearing years commence; it is indeed a time of waiting anew. The woman waits each month again, but this time, for signs of conception; once achieved, however, her waiting is hardly past. The expectant mother now waits the nine months for her womb to issue the child forth. In this modern medically controlled society we often forget this part; as doctor controlled as the process has become – it is still a waiting game. And this is more true for the woman, herself, than anyone else – regardless of how close others remain in the picture. After all, it is she who conceived, carried the baby, and then she who will have to labor, and then raise the child.

The waiting game hardly ends, though, at birth; each day, each week, month and year of the growing child's existence requires a new kind of waiting for the mother. Just as the mother once looked for signs of fecundity, then signs of conception, then finally labor; now the mother looks for signs of development – for readiness – if you will. Is the infant raising his head, is she turning over, is she ready for solid foods, is he ready for toilet training; and this goes on for years.

It is a natural process and the waiting game is very much a part of it. Men are being inserted into all areas of formerly feminized territory. At home they change diapers and wash dishes. At work they become nurses and pre-school teachers. Emotionally they have been called upon to develop deeper introspection and responsiveness to others' needs. Regardless of the merits of these changes, men have remained men. Near as we know, these changes have not changed the basic DNA. Women still do the conceiving.

In the tremendous societal thrust to even out the gender roles, some seem to have come to imagine that we can de-sex human beings - to make us all androgynous. One wonders how we would then attract one another – or is that no longer of importance?!!

Leave that thinking behind for a moment.

For the moment, at least, men and women appear to have remained men and women. And perhaps, as such a politically correct society, we might want to question why it is we are so keen on changing that. Surely we don't all have gender confusion issues. Clearly the majority, or so psychology assumes, are comfortable in their gender suits, so to speak. What then is the great turmoil?

Women leave the house, much like men each morning. Yes, they do tend to have the greater child rearing roles; but they did bear these children – an intimate closeness that no man will seemingly ever know. These women are doctors, lawyers, professors, engineers, CEOs; they work long days doing what men have always done. The children are now far away from both parents day after day. Women have achieved much of what men have always had. They can work endlessly, thanklessly, and sometimes even heartlessly just like men. And yet these executives are still women. Biology still requires that they wait, month after month, year after year.

Freud, a misogynist – if there ever was one – described biology as destiny. It was his downcast outlook on the female gender. What Freud failed to see was the positives. In learning how to wait, women have been given an ability almost completely peculiar to them. It's what made so many of them the wonderful teachers and nurses that society came to love. It's what made them capable mothers, as well. I, too, am a woman – a proud one – perhaps this is my time to wait for society – and women especially – to come to a more positive outlook on their femininity. As a woman, I've waited for many things. I guess that I can wait for this, as well.

A Wellness of Mind

For two weeks of my life I was imprisoned by my body within my mind or perhaps it was really by my mind within my body; the difference of which I may have to mill over for a long time now. I had innocently gone to see my long time physician over something I thought rather minor, only to find that he thought otherwise. Somehow a check up became several tests, machines, and then a call to the hospital - I was scheduled for Friday. Truth be known - he gave me choice - wait or do it now - wait meant not knowing - I needed to know NOW - Today - YESTERDAY.

For the next few days I had left the world and curled up - but not comfortably - inside my psyche. My whole world became my body. I carried out my obligations, made necessary plans, and told only the two people who had to know; even my daughters went untold.

Thursday night passed unto Friday mercilessly slowly. Arriving at the hospital, I was entered into the industry of same day surgery - it was routine for them - but not for me. I was to meet one very caring anesthetist - incidentally not mine - as well as one recovery nurse who was more involved in her evening plans than my desperation to get out. On a whole, people were kind - care in a world of HMOs and third world backwardness, were all but forgotten in this small private hospital in affluent American suburbia. I propelled myself out of the obligatory wheelchair and, a little weak kneed, sank into my son and daughter-in-law's car - I had been set free.

But the freedom was to be short-lived. As eagerly as I met my daughters (the younger just home from college) and as eagerly as I retook ownership of my belongings - my life still appeared over the horizon - fuzzy and unsure. The findings - the pathologist's report - were good - but still no key appeared - I languished still deep within my strangling cocoon. Two weeks after the initial visit I returned to the office - I thought they were going to have to pick me up off the ceiling - when I heard that he wanted to examine me again - wasn't the procedure - the hospitalization - the whole bloody ordeal enough - was there no end to this nightmare?

In the end it seemed that this wasn't an examination, it was a treatment for something he hadn't even mentioned at the initial visit - something he had only waved off ten years back. It seems he couldn't treat it until he knew that everything was negative; but that was small relief - for me - the patient - the soul behind the tissue. Afterwards, he would kid me as he always had before. When I asked him for the umpteenth time - if I was really okay - if I could really retake my life - he said to "Go home and make my middle child's wedding". He offered to have his receptionist type it up for me - she looked at me waiting to see my response - I told her that it wasn't necessary. But was it - what would it have done - I'm still not sure.

Now, yet another week passed that blackened Tuesday, I still find myself sledgehammering my way out. Butterflies, too struggle with theirs; but theirs is a natural strife - one of growth and maturation - mine is one of fear - and medical molestation. Oh, this is not to say that I found my doctor unprofessional - no, he did his job – but job and all, I am more than the questionable tissues which had to be examined and repaired; and it is far more difficult to anesthetize or cauterize the mind than the body.

Some nights now I can sleep - dreams no longer continually filled with blood and death or black and dying; but I am still suspicious of my innocent body. For although it did nothing wrong - it stands accused at every twitch at every creak - I fear it as much as I had once feared the hospital and the instruments. Having always been a champion

of nature and nature as medicine and all knowing - it leaves me with less

of a sense of who I am and what I am about.

I have, however, become rapidly aware of the chipping away at

the body-trusting mechanisms of women my age - women in their forties.

I have opened my eyes to find my friends, neighbors and colleagues with

ugly scabs from mole removals, prescriptions to 'replace' all the

elements that are supposedly being lost by their forty-plus bodies, and

watching their every move to see if they 'require' this test or this action.

I feel in all objectivity, that my procedure was probably advisable; but I

wonder about this medical onslaught against women of my age. One

would think that one was dying one right after another. I, also, wonder

when forty became the age of the great medical Big Brother, certainly

my mother thought herself young at that time - now that we are living

longer has forty become somehow older? It scares me to read how some

women are electing to undergo mastectomies in fear of the possibility

that breast cancer may one day occur. It scares me to watch my friends

go for one doctor visit after the other and one invasive test after another -

simply because they've reached a certain age - our age. I watched

hypochondria all my waking life; my mother - she should be well - was

always dragging herself and my father and us to some doctor. I've always wondered if my background of yeast infections and my daughter's early allergic reaction to penicillin stem from all the antibiotics she had doctors feed us. There was always something physically wrong with her or one of us and it was always something only a doctor could fix. A cool cloth, some hot soup, or a warm blanket were never sufficient - we always required medical help. My and my children's lives of midwifery - few antibiotics - and doctors who tend to talk more than touch, are no doubt, a rebound reaction from my childhood overwhelm with the medical world and my nature hating mother. And yet I would not take back a nature respecting second of my life; I am just finding it harder to return.

Somewhere out there - or perhaps somewhere within - is the healing scalpel to finally cut myself loose from the cocooned depression that still encompasses me. Perhaps then I can better deal with what it means to be a forty-something woman in the year two thousand; and then my nature loving - respecting place in it. Until then there is no healing, because just as the doctor could not promise me what I really wanted to hear, which was to 'go have a nice life and don't bother coming back'; my own equilibrium with finding my own fit in all this, is not necessarily the rose garden I always chose it to be. Forty is older than twenty. Bodies do change. Nature sometimes does need some help. Of course change isn't necessarily bad. How much help and when is help not necessarily helpful? And how do you know the difference? Some of the answers surely could come from the medical books; but my guess is that the greater ones come from ourselves and how much we want to be responsible for our own bodies and our own lives. Just as no doctor can promise you one hundred twenty years of life; no life style can promise such longevity equally well. All the tests in the world will not stop your hair from greying, your shape from shifting, and your cells from aging. Therefore part of the answer may lie in one's own idea of life quality. Do you feel safer under the medical camera's eye - or your own? Do you feel safer downing some hormones and calcium supplements or would you prefer herbal tea, diet, or nothing at all? Would you rather watch yourself for signs of the need for medical intervention; or are you afraid that by then it may be too late? How much of your life are you willing to give up to doctors' lounges, machines, or in potential worry of the unknown? All these must be personal questions - decisions I would want to make for no one other than me. But the options, as imperfect as they are, leave me feeling that options exist; normal life may be out there for the choosing and taking. I may have to accept that lack of life assurance - that at the end all will be fine - if I keep to my soft and fuzzy regimen of natural respect and tenderness; but the doctors are promising us no more. For now my cocoon still blurs my eyes and mind to the ramifications of our questions and answers. While with each and every Tuesday reached, I can begin to make myself out in the distance as a survivor of sorts; and maybe then decide into what kind of a world I want to spend this chance I've been given - at least for now.

Working People

Ever look at your fellow commuter and wonder what makes him tick? Does he appear angry? Does she appear distracted? Is there one man in your train station each morning who never says good morning? Another who won't stop talking? What's your working posture consist of? Do you hurry off to work in the morning? Are you excited or scared, moody, annoyed, or just too depressed to care?

The twenty-first century has found adults working more hours, more days per week, more holidays, and more years than the mid twentieth century would have predicted. When I was growing up, the predictions were of a four day week. Now with labor unions having taken an enormous step back and the economy making a nose dive, so many people are simply not making it! Add that to the fact that most people do not work in jobs or fields they're happy in; and you're got a very ugly picture of a bulk of the hours of the average adult's life.

Oh, of course there are some people who get up each morning, thankfully, in love with their careers. I think of a Unitarian Minister and

Orthodox Rabbi, I know well. I think of several teachers and small business owners as well. My children's pediatrician was certainly one of them. But most adults, including myself – working to support myself so I can actually do the writing and research I so love - are to some degree miserable at work. We drag ourselves there each day, have that same terrified Sunday night feeling, as we did as children not looking forward to school, and count the minutes and hours until our cherished freedom each night.

Most people take this misery for granted, never questioning it or even trying to make a change.

The origin of some of the misery is parents. Many people simply ended up in fields their parents scripted for them. I know adults whose entire education was parent directed to secure them the careers the parents decided they belonged in. This scripting in some cases raises its ugly heads in middle age, after the parents had either passed on or no longer matter in that way; and then some of these BRAVE people reeducate themselves to become WHAT THEY WANTED TO BE ALL ALONG.

Many however, just happened into their line of work out of need or misreading or second guessing themselves. Some may never have seen any choices along the way.

What is it about work, after all, that has the power to make us so miserable? Have you ever thought about that? Most people don't allow much else in their lives to make them as miserable as work does. Why is that? A lot of it is need based. While most of us will only put up with so much from our neighbors, relatives, or anyone else for that matter, work in many cases, leaves us almost on prisoner status. We enter each morning (or afternoon, evening, or night depending on your hours) almost like small school children. We keep trying to keep our noses clean, while killing ourselves to stay ahead. The bosses, supervisors, and overseers take on the role of punitive parents, teachers, prison guards, and probation officers. They're the continual police presence in our lives; creating, in many cases, unremitting fear.

Sometimes in our misery, we negate the thought of lessening the misery in our own situation or leaving the situation; we're even more likely to forget that our fellow commuter is, in all probability, suffering too.

Furthermore, did you ever wonder what it is about work that disturbs us so? I mean is it waking up early, the drudgery, the time away from loved ones, loved things, or loved pastimes, or is it merely the ever present BOSS? Actually the source of the misery is the stealing of your soul. We handle all kinds of crazy hours for our loved ones, adored pastimes, and cherished keepsakes. We wake up in the middle of the night for infants, stay up till dawn waiting for prodigal teenagers, or run out to catch the first fish or the first ray of 'dawn's early light'. We spend tremendous energy waxing the car we never thought we'd be able to buy, or cutting the lawn in front of the house for which we saved more than a decade, we accept time away from our loved ones to see that fantastic play, to bowl, to visit a friend........................ No, it's all much more than that, it's the desperate attempt to steal our collective souls.

There is a legendary picture of the middle/upper middle class father of lore coming home. Mommy quickly shoos away the kids, kisses him, accompanies him to his armchair, supplying him with his slippers, pipe and all, and then fetching him a drink. She then disappears from view. This isn't about alcoholism, folks; this about the desperate attempt to keep his soul. All day long he fought to keep it. He fought to keep it against the company at large, against his customers, against his competing coworkers, and ultimately from his boss. After all that fight, there's simply nothing left. He needs to be strengthened, bulwarked to handle tomorrow's battle.

There are ancient Biblically based stories on how the Israelite women kept their husbands alive during the Egyptian slavery. How they fed them and comforted them; the unsaid lines were so they could continue the race. What they were really doing were saving their husbands' souls.

Today we look around us on that train and we're surrounded with probably almost as many, if not more, women than men. Are women subjected to this as well, you query? Hell, yes. Women have been sold a bill of goods when it came to career above family. Oh, this is not to say that women shouldn't have the same opportunities; just that the lie was that the workforce was superior! Life in the workforce isn't superior to childraising, to family investments, to running your own homebased life; it's inferior. It keeps you away from those you love and does it's very best to tear you up and spit you out. Oh children can be difficult, spouses, no less; but they don't steal your soul. They don't attempt to coerce you to do anything or everything to keep that job to 'get ahead', to 'please' that ignorant supervisor or boss, to compete with that idiot coworker. It can be boring to sweep that floor, it can be tedious to buy those groceries, and potty training can seem like more than you bargained for some days – but at the end of the day you don't feel robbed – You're still you.

We're not accustomed to seeing work as a negative. Adler, one of the legendary trio who fathered modern psychoanalysis, saw work as a basic part of the human makeup, as something the makes us what we are. But what kind of work? Certainly the farmer, the small business owner, the physician (presuming he/she isn't doing it to please mom) may feel that his or her work is part of her /his make up. But this is not true with the salesman from the car dealership, this is not true of the adjuster for the insurance company, this is not true for the assembly line factory worker. The assembly line worker was actually the source of a study not so many decades ago, it showed that when the assembly line worker just handled one part of the enormous car production, that he was much more inclined to become impotent. Now why is that? It's because if we're forced to earn our bread, as we have been since the time of Adam and Eve, that we need it to be a meaningful effort, not like the Greek story of moving the rock up and down for naught in prison, but to build the entire car, not just add one screw. When you plow your field you're exhausted but you know in the big picture that you're growing food, not just for your family but for your neighbors and customers. You know that the crops will fill your family's stomachs and provide money to purchase the heating fuel and other necessities and niceties your family deems necessary. Perhaps you see some of this as an employee, too, but it's almost completely eclipsed when you're lied to and robbed of your dignity and ultimately of your soul. My current daytime employer tells his employees when they're warm or cold enough and even outright lies about occurrences from the day or minute before. People subjected to this continual practice are being robbed, not just of their sanity, but of their very souls. It's impossible not to react to this type of maltreatment.

We live in a highly competitive world. Hispanic girls have been reported to have committed suicide after observing the tremendous gap between life on TV and life in their tenement existence. Most of us are not that far ahead. Not only must we buy That vehicle, That house, That electronic device; but we've become convinced that without these things we are not fully complete. We work absurdly long hours giving up holidays, family time, and loved pursuits to buy things for our families and selves. We're not the farmer, here, however, we're not merely feeding our children's bellies and keeping the house warm; we're selling our souls for granite countertops. Those granite countertops will be here long after we're gone and what difference could they possibly make?

Years ago in my first REAL job after high school, I was asked, upon the company finding out that I write, why I didn't want to write for them; I knew then as very much as I know today –I didn't want anyone to tell me how or what to write. That's a very long time ago, but nothing has changed. In spending an eon studying Psychology, I opened a small practice only to find something very strange. I had ADORED pro bono counseling; I HATED fee for service. In fee for service you had to watch that clock. In fee for service, your clientele expected you to perform emotional miracles for their fees rather than seeing the professional relationship as a working process. I stopped practicing.

Each individual has to decide for him or herself what he or she is willing to sell in order to pay Paul or Peter. This can't be your mother's decision. It can't even be your spouse's. It certainly shouldn't be your offspring's. Even in earning just enough to raise my family and finally to do my writing and research, I've spent far too much time and energy working for 'the man'. I'm not sorry that I never made much money, I only detest the time spent involved in such meaningless toil. You have to choose your own path, just be aware that there are choices and alternate life styles. They may not be your family's style, they may not make you look big at your school's twenty-fifth reunion; BUT do any of these things REALLY MATTER? I spoke to someone recently, who chose to become an artist even though his school advisors strongly cautioned him against it. He has done well; but he proudly says that he was willing to go hungry for the cause. And cause it is indeed. It's a cause called soul.

Friskie

If I don't write this poem,

No one will ever know your name;

Although you were kind, loving, smart and brave,

Because you could not write, speak, build, paint, or sing

a note.

But please let it be known,

That you left your paw upon our hearts;

And we will never be the same.

Not the Status Quo

I don't think I thought about it all that much, nor completely appreciated the situation until its loss. But each work evening, now, as I board the bus, I am well aware of how fortunate I, indeed, was.

Commuting is not usually considered something to wax eloquently or tearfully maudlin about, but that is what I am finding myself doing. Having recently relocated, due to the necessity for me to lessen my formerly lengthy work hours to part time and move in with my children, as my disability worsens, I find myself waiting on line for a bus; where there are no saved seats, and while the traveling time is quicker, the warmth, kindness, and concern are all behind me.

Oh, my old route did not commence that way. It took me a while to find the right train at the right time; and then one unusually caring conductor, to point to the first car, where I would not have to climb down the stairs at my destination.

That act of kindness, led me to a car of strangers, who became my travel family and friends. One rider shepherded us all, by having us meet in one area, where he would find out the boarding track information before it was listed on the departure board; therefore permitting us comfortable, no shoving passage, to the train. Once there, we shared a car, where even if we did not know everyone's name, we KNEW them. We talked and inquired and cared for one another. One woman would even become a very good friend.

Today I find myself working one to two days less a week, sleeping more, feeling better, but mourning all these special people's company. I've even been told that they ask for me.

Given the perspective of time, it's sometimes amazing what we find ourselves missing. Unbeknownst to the materialists, it frequently is not the 'stuff' money can buy. Here I am freed of some of the traditional working and commuting drudgery, finding myself missing that special commute and those VERY SPECIAL commuters. I'm not mourning the financial loss; although it worries my family at large, as they fear me as an impending burden. I'm not mourning workplace perks, reserved for full time employees. I'm not even mourning the feeling of being able to work as hard and as long as I have to, to survive. I'm mourning a train car full of individuals, I grew to love.

In time, I will surely swallow deeply and let this go too, much as we accept the many losses that confront adulthood; and yet that doesn't lessen the special caring community that I was once a part. Closure is an ideal that frequently eludes us in the 'real' adult world. A commuter sees the same rider day after day and then one day he is no longer there. What happened to him? Did he fall ill? Did he lose his job? Did he die? Frequently we just never find out. As a somewhat shy and introverted individual, I never even said good-bye to all my commuter friends. Partially it was the mixed feelings I had about my exit, my move; going from self sufficient adult to an obviously disabled one, moving in with relatives. Partially it was the lifelong distaste of bringing notice to myself; i.e. I came in quietly, I will leave the same way. Only thing is, the exit is never quite the same, for whatever took place, has changed you, probably forever.

And so each work evening, I look for that continuum that fails to appear. Oh, perhaps a substitute commuter family will arise; I just doubt it somehow.

A Few Thoughts on our Civil Rights

I believe it was Benjamin Franklin who said that "Those who give up essential liberty to purchase a little temporary safety, deserve neither liberty nor safety". That may have been some two hundred years back, but little has changed.

We live in a time of McCarthyism revisited. The government is causing fear in the American citizenry at large, in order to remove our social freedoms, our civil rights. Each and every lessening of our freedom depriving us from being who we are, doing what we feel is right to do, doing what our consciences ache for. Our Constitutional freedoms of liberty, life, and the pursuit of happiness are being excused with a wave of the judicial hand, claiming that it's all about protection – protection indeed – but what is it that we're being protected from? The 'Evil Immigrant'? More likely we're being protected from ourselves. As citizens, we're seen as problematic; but in the name of Security, if you take away our social rights, then the government can order us around, much like a bunch of toy soldiers..................Marching as ordered without gripe or question...................

There is, in addition, a second type of social rights lessening going on. This is in the name of protection of children and personal health. There are such referenda as for the illegalization of an adult smoking in a car with his/her children present – sounds good – or does it? Whenever a schizophrenic commits a crime there are legislation suggested to make taking medication the law – sounds great doesn't it? Currently, if you're impoverished and especially if you're accepting any government financial assistance, there are laws that can remove children from your custody if you spank them – sounds wonderful doesn't it?

Well, what is going on here, you query. Is the government protecting us or not? Well, the answer isn't as simple as it sounds. Let's look at the questions closer. If you're a child and your parent insists on holding your hand while you cross the street – That's fine – That's a parent's duty; but if you're thirty-five and the government snaps handcuffs on you to make sure that you cross the street THEIR WAY – that's something different.

In the anti-immigrant legislation – (Well, it's not pro-immigrant is it – how could throwing immigrants out be PRO) - the American public is being made fearful day and night. In train and bus stations and airports nationwide, the public is repeatedly reminded to look for suspicious baggage or items or made to stand on lines exhibiting endless pieces of identification or even being searched or scanned largely in the name of the 'dangerous immigrant'.

In the social health and parenting legislation, Uncle Sam has taken on the hat of Big Brother, instructing the public on better health and parenting. The only problem being, that there is rarely one way to skin a cat; and instructing is one thing, legislating is another. I have enough relatives – THANK YOU – I don't need Big Brother!!!

For those who wonder what's wrong with limiting the second hand smoke received by children or the pummeling their backsides may receive, or force medicating the mentally ill, try going a little further. For one thing the government is standing in between parents and children – Who gave them that right? Who made legislators physicians in deciding who Must take highly dangerous psychiatric medication? Secondly, while one might think that those legislations are so healthful that they're worth coercion, one better look at steps two and three. If you're buying the first steps, are you prepared to buy the ones that follow? If you're against smoking, unmedicated emotionally ill, and spanking, are you also against coffee, fats, sugar, chocolate, R or X rated movies; who is to know where it is to end? I'll tell you where it's to end

– with the very denial of your freedoms – your very right to life, liberty, and the pursuit of freedom.

Needless to say, these social entanglements will affect the poor first – laws almost always do – firstly because they are more visual, secondly because they're usually less sophisticated (on the whole, except for artists and writers), and thirdly because they cannot afford the legal system designed to protect them. Secondly, what have you bought in this rights for security bargain – Do you feel safer? Have you any solid proof of your safety, better health, or better parenting skills? And will you draw no line? What if the government decides that they can bring up your children in a superior manner to you – will you open the door for them – Different government agencies do this to the poor all the time.

If you're affluent, you will probably be safer – at least for a while – but as more and more of your social liberties are stripped away – you are sure to be effected at some point. Also, if you're an artist, a homosexual, labeled mentally ill, or in anyway individualistic, you are liable to be in more danger in both the social and security oriented legislation - remember the famous words of Martin Niemoeller

"First they came for the Communists

But I was not a Communist

So I did not speak out.

Then they came for the Socialists and the Trade Unionists

But I was not one of them,

So I did not speak out.

Then they came for the Jews

But I was not Jewish

So I did not speak out.

Then they came for me,

There was no one left to speak out for me."

Just remember – it could be you.

Scandinavia has long stood out as a liberal socialist region, but let's take a closer look. True, if you're a young adult with individualist mode of dress and coiffure, and even with a penchant for the occasional 'recreational drug use', you'll probably be left alone. Should you desire to pay for state sanctioned sexual favors, you, too, will remain untouched by the law. But let's dig a little deeper, if you will, try marrying someone from outside your nation – WHOOPS – you may have to live with your mate in a nation other than your own. If your homeland is Denmark, you may have to wait six months after your baby is born to find out if your government accepts your child's proposed name. The reasons behind both legalities, sound sensible, protective, and socially wise, but are they? The limitation on immigration is based on economics, a nation has to be able to afford those individuals it accepts into its borders. Names can be a source of much teasing and bullying in childhood. But how do we feel about the enactments, the legislations of these social visions? You're born and raised in one country, but lo and behold when you marry a member of another nation – the two of you can't live there as a union? You bring a child into the world, but it's your government who makes the decision on what you can call her or him? These may well sound like pages out of an Orwellian novel, but they're not, they're actual laws.

The U.S., rightly or wrongly, is no Scandinavia. If you drove around with long hair and hippy garb in the sixties and seventies, your car was likely to be stopped. Recreational drug use, rightly or wrongly, continues to be vigorously pursued. Even Post New Deal, we've never labeled ourselves as anything but a Capitalistic, Democratic Union; but the social laws are abounding and perhaps we should take a better look at them before they control us.

Protection and control are always viewed differently, that is when the proverbial shoe is on the other foot. Take the proposal of taking away the poor's rights to buy soda with food stamps. Well, after all WE taxpayers pay for the stamps; why should THEY waste them on poor nutritionally, high sugar items? Okay, but the poor pay taxes, as well, proportionally less, of course; but they do pay taxes. Every time they purchase a taxed item from a legal retailer, taxes are paid. Every time they work legally, taxes are paid, etc., etc.... What if our ever protective legislators decide tomorrow to take all carbonated sweetened beverages out of the market, is that alright, too? After all soda is no better for the middle or affluent classes than it is for the poor. What's source for the goose isn't for the gander? Frankly, I'll keep my Coca Cola under my mattress, my only fear is that it's liable to become more and more lumpy as chocolate, coffee, and sugar are slowly delegalized. I'd make a Great ExPat, but where would I go; and would you like to join me, too?

Before giving our legislators the power to play Big Brother, take a deep breath, and ponder carefully upon the Great Franklin's words, as we, too, may end up with neither liberty nor safety.

Handicapped By Any Other Name

I have never been politically correct. I say this from the outset, because it will save us a lot of trouble in the long run. I have succeeded in insulting professors, colleagues, friends, relatives, and who knows how many other innocent individuals, because of the lack of this very disclaimer.

The other evening, listening to the radio (my favourite medium) I grew slowly annoyed, if not actually angry. The subject was disabilities, the disabled, and whether the American Disabilities Act (1990) has made the lives of the disabled, and families, better. I listened carefully. After all, I have a learning disabled daughter. After all, I have worked with the disabled (mentally, physically, and academically) for well over as decade. I listened carefully. But what I didn't hear was whether the lives of these individuals became better or not. What I heard was something quite different.

I heard that it was still very difficult for some of the disabled to achieve independence through the securing of income earning jobs. I heard about the frustration of those individuals (or their families) involved with sheltered workshop jobs. I heard how the disabled are sometimes subject to prejudice on the basis of certain disabilities over other disabilities.

I did not hear how children, throughout this great land, are now unilaterally educated regardless of their disability. I did not hear of how workplaces and public places, of all kinds, are being designed (or redesigned) for ready access for the disabled. I did not hear how employers are encouraged to make all sorts of accommodations for the disabled. I did not hear of how street corners and most modes of transportation have been redesigned with this very population in mind. I did not hear that each and every institution of higher learning is supposed to devote time, energy, and funds in order to allow every disabled student to achieve, if at all possible.

But what I missed hearing most in this particular broadcast - were just those words - *if at all possible*. Why? Why did I miss those very words. Because this broadcast, dedicated to the disabled, was in itself disabled. This, after all, was not a broadcast of then and now - to see how far the disabled have come in this brief decade; that, indeed, would have been a broadcast of the possible. What my ears had been treated to (if you want to call it that) was a broadcast of the impossible.

Individuals whose disabilities are far too serious to permit for mainstreamed work are fortunate to be able to fall back on the sheltered workshops. Not all societies possess such a luxury. Indeed the cost of labor must far exceed production. Furthermore, I was almost speechless as to the explanation of the *hierarchy* of disabilities. I was informed that at the very bottom of this, very involved, enumeration were those individuals with intellectual disabilities.

I thought back at that time - to a good friend, whose now grown son, is very slightly hearing impaired. I remember, not long ago, how she described crying over this terrible loss. Then she added, *wisely,* that she then visited a friend of hers who had several small children - all completely bereft of hearing. The difference between her story (sad as it was) and the one painted on the radio, is the difference those four little words make - *if at all possible.*

No matter how sad it is, some individuals will always be too disabled to work in the mainstream. Some will even be too disabled to work in sheltered workshops. No matter how sad it is, some individuals are intellectually handicapped; saying that this is sad, does not change the facts. Although the American Disabilities Act (1990) did not solve all the practical problems of the disabled; it did go a long way in making an important effort. However, law can only perform the possible. Law cannot take away the disabilities nature created.

Soup and Bread

I was thinking tonight, as I tenderly dipped my bread into my soup and savoured it, how safe that has always made me feel; and how far back that feeling went.............

I was newly married, very poor, and living on a military base, with another family. We were at the end of the month and there simply was nothing left in the refrigerator or cupboards. L-rd alone knows what the other couple's children subsisted on; though I have a vague memory of that unpalatable powdered milk. Having jointly spent the entire food funds for the month, I went through my meagre belongings and found a dollar and change. Running to the commissary, as if I had struck gold, I brought back a single loaf of bread and a box of powdered noodle soup mix. I think I will forever remember the taste of the bread dipped lovingly into that soup.

Although, I've come a long way since that day, becoming quite a 'foodie' at one point, there is nothing that makes me feel quite as satiated as dipping bread into soup. It can be any kind of soup and any type of bread; the magic remains the same.

It's an odd thing about food, as food is so much more than the mere sum of its parts. Bread is so much more than flour and water, soup more than water and vegetables, chocolate more than its rich cocoa origin. Hot food not only warms our inners, it warms our very being. Sometime the food eaten at day's end is all that I have to make me feel warm, safe, and satiated. A meal with a friend is not quite like anything else. A feast with family is the stuff from which legends are made.

All religions celebrate with food. Food was offered to the G-ds* as a peace offering, as well as a gift of thanks! We bake goodies and dress them up, giving them to friends and relatives. We go out to unabashedly pricey eateries to celebrate the times in our lives or pay even costlier caterers, to come to us to cook and serve.

My youngest daughter once said, in describing Thanksgiving growing up, that it was all about the food; and while I would say that it many ways it was all about our thankfulness, one could equally say that it was the food that rendered us so grateful...............

Having been hungry, so early in life, I always find others' hunger pangs mirrored deeply within my own gut. Once hunger becomes real to you, you're not likely to ever forget the plight.

Indeed, I understand overeating, (although I, myself, remain slim) closeted eating, and even stealing food. It's anorexia, except in a professional or theoretical sense, that remains lost on me!

Poverty tears at you in ways that never completely heal. I remember my son, when he was still in college, complaining that he couldn't afford milkshakes. As for me, the lowest point of poverty effecting myself alone, was one Sunday, walking through the streets looking for change, longing to buy the New York Times. Alas, there was no change, in my corner of suburbia. My children were too young to understand at the time and I probably never told them what I went out to do. They had food, but I went hungry for my mind..............

Recently, on a visit to my youngest daughter's abode, I joyously saw her very full refrigerator and made a blessing that she may never know anything else.............................

I remember when I first started job hunting, depriving myself of lunch, so that I would just keep going nonstop. I saw food as a reward, that I would have to earn. I had no idea back then, how hard I would have to work to earn it.

Today I continue to labor for my daily bread and The New York Times. I, also continue to lovingly dip my beloved bread into my wondrous soup and continue to respond in awe………………………

* As a researcher into Comparative Religious Thought, I've always proclaimed : Who are we to say that someone else's deity doesn't begin with an uppercase 'g'.

Renee Ducker is a graduate of the State University of New York. A
writer and researcher of Comparative Religious Thought, Mrs. Ducker
served as a bit of a Renaissance Woman / a 'Jill' of all trades in
supporting her three children; playing such roles as retail department
manager, trouble shooter, counselor, private school educator and
administrator, camp administrator, Ethics teacher, proofreader and editor,
and operations supervisor in the business world. Then, in her late
fifties, she shocked her world by marrying a retired Psychotherapist from
West Virginia.